Praise for Barbara Garson's

DOWN THE UP ESCALATOR

"Americans cope with the fallout from forty years of dwindling prospects in this quietly harrowing mosaic of economic decline. . . . Garson's vivid, shrewd, warmly sympathetic profiles show the resilience with which ordinary Americans respond to misfortune, but also the enduring costs as they abandon hopes for a fulfilling career, an extra child, or a secure retirement. The result is a compelling portrait of an economy that has turned against the people."

—*Publishers Weekly* (starred review)

"Garson is the perfect person to write a book about economic injustice. . . . Her book of stories is a convincing effort to show that the recession was part of ongoing restructuring—a restructuring at least partially motivated by greed—that is making it hard for many Americans to ride *up* the economic escalator." —*The Christian Science Monitor*

"Barbara Garson has written a small masterpiece of wise and alarming reportage about how ordinary Americans are surviving during extraordinarily rotten times. *Down the Up Escalator* is a necessary antidote to all the blather about 'freeing' banks and investment houses from 'crippling regulations.'" —Michael Kazin, author of

American Dreamers:
How the Left Changed a Nation

"That sense of human connection and care is woven through Garson's compelling rendition of the economic story we've come to know so well, the squeeze not just on people at the bottom but people who were—or at least thought they were—in the middle, as well. . . . Garson's curious eye and warm presence throughout the book create a sense of connection rather than hopelessness."   —*Daily Kos*

"Years from now, when historians want to know what it was really like to live during this recession, they'll find no better place to look than Garson's book."   —John B. Judis, Senior Editor, *The New Republic,* and Visiting Scholar, The Carnegie Endowment for International Peace

"This book is a compassionate, probing, pointillist mural of the Great Recession and of the decades-long erosion of the average American's economic position that preceded it, all told through the experiences of individual men and women. She has followed some over time, has sought out others whose lives illuminate larger injustices, and has found people whose stories will stick with you."
—Adam Hochschild, author of *King Leopold's Ghost*

"In this evocative book, Barbara Garson hears out a host of victims, gamblers, and scramblers ensnared in the network of rackets that drives the American economy, and shows how high-level policies produce collateral damage and blast dreams. This is reporting for hearts and minds alike."
—Todd Gitlin, author of *Occupy Nation: The Roots, the Spirit, and the Promise of Occupy Wall Street*

Barbara Garson

DOWN THE UP ESCALATOR

Barbara Garson is the author of three books: *All the Livelong Day: The Meaning and Demeaning of Routine Work*, *The Electronic Sweatshop*, and most recently *Money Makes the World Go Around: One Investor Tracks Her Cash Through the Global Economy*. She has also written several plays, including *MacBird!* and OBIE award–winning *The Dinosaur Door* and her work has appeared in *Harper's*, *The New York Times*, *Newsweek*, and *The Nation*.

Also by Barbara Garson

Books

*Money Makes the World Go Around: One Investor
Tracks Her Cash Through the Global Economy*

*The Electronic Sweatshop: How Computers Are Transforming
the Office of the Future into the Factory of the Past*

*All the Livelong Day: The Meaning and
Demeaning of Routine Work*

Plays

Mac Bird!

Going Co-op

The Dinosaur Door

The Department

Security

DOWN THE UP ESCALATOR

How the 99 Percent Live

BARBARA GARSON

Anchor Books

A Division of Random House LLC

New York

FIRST ANCHOR BOOKS EDITION, JANUARY 2014

Copyright © 2013 by Barbara Garson

All rights reserved. Published in the United States by Anchor Books, a division of Random House LLC, New York, and in Canada by Random House of Canada Limited, Toronto, Penguin Random House Companies. Originally published in hardcover in the United States by Doubleday, a division of Random House LLC, New York, 2013.

Anchor Books and colophon are registered trademarks of Random House LLC.

"The Mystery of the Missing Unemployed Man" was previously published in slightly different form on TomDispatch.com.

The Library of Congress has cataloged the Doubleday edition as follows:
Garson, Barbara.
Down the up escalator : how the 99 percent live in the Great
Recession / Barbara Garson.
p. cm.
1. Income distribution—United States—History—21st century.
2. Equality—United States—History—21st century.
3. Global Financial Crisis, 2008–2009. I. Title.
HC110.I5G376 2013
339.2'20973—dc23
2012020359

Anchor Books Trade Paperback ISBN: 978-0-307-47598-5
eBook ISBN: 978-0-385-53275-4

Author photograph © Frank Leonard
Book design by Michael Collica

www.anchorbooks.com

Printed in the United States of America
10 9 8 7 6 5 4 3 2 1

CONTENTS

III: OUR SAVINGS

AUTHOR'S NOTE

In order to protect the identities of most of the people I interviewed for this book, I did not use their real names. Money is such a sensitive subject that I eventually changed all names except for a couple of people who spoke in their official capacities and one media-savvy fellow whose own blog reveals far more intimate things about him than I do here. I also changed the location of a small town, and I regretfully concealed a few corporate names that it would have been fun to mention. Despite these bits of camouflage, none of the people you're about to meet are composites. They're individuals speaking in their own words.

DOWN THE UP ESCALATOR

INTRODUCTION

What Caused the Great Recession (in Three Scenes and One Phone Call)

I met a man about forty years ago and caught up with him on three more occasions. These four scenes, spanning four decades of his life, should have been enough for me to predict the Great Recession. But I didn't put it together till now.

SCENE I

In the late 1960s I worked at a coffeehouse near an army base from which soldiers shipped out to Vietnam. A lot of the GIs who frequented our place were putting out antiwar newspapers and planning demonstrations—one group was even organizing a union inside the army.

But I often sat with a young man back from Vietnam who was simply waiting out the time till his discharge. Duane had floppy brown hair, lively eyes, a sweet smile, and was slightly buck-toothed. He was handy and would fix our record player or show up with a part that made our old mimeograph machine run more smoothly.

He rarely spoke about the war except to say that his company stayed stoned the whole time. "Our motto was 'Let's not and say we did.' Me and this other guy painted that on a big banner. It stayed up for a whole day," he noted with a mix of sardonic and genuine pride.

That was the extent of Duane's antiwar activism. He didn't intend to become a professional Vietnam vet like John Kerry. His plan was to return to Cleveland and make up for time missed in the civilian counterculture.

I enjoyed my breaks with Duane because of his warm, self-aware humor, but thousands of GIs passed through the coffeehouse, and I didn't particularly notice when he left.

SCENE II

In the early 1970s General Motors set up the fastest auto assembly line in the world in Lordstown, Ohio, and staffed it with workers whose average age was twenty-four.

The management hoped that these healthy, young, and inexperienced workers would handle 101 cars an hour without balking the way longtime autoworkers surely would have. But the pace and monotony were just as oppressive to the younger workers. What GM got at Lordstown instead of balkiness, however, was a series of slowdowns and snafus aimed at the speed of the line. The management publicized this as systematic "sabotage"—until it realized that that could hurt car sales.

I visited Lordstown the week before a strike vote, amid national speculation about the generation of "hippie autoworkers" whose talk about "humanizing the assembly line" was supposed to change forever the way America works.

On a guided tour of the plant (how else could I get inside?), I spotted Duane shooting radios into cars with an air gun. We recognized each other, but in the regimented factory environment we both instinctively thought it better not to let on. In lieu of a greeting, Duane slipped me a note with his phone number. At home that evening he summarized life since his discharge.

"Remember you guys gave me a giant banana split the day I ETSed [got out as scheduled]. Well, it's been downhill since then. I came back to Cleveland, stayed with my dad, who was unemployed. Man, was that ever a downer. But I figured things would pick up if I got wheels, so I got a car. But it turned out the car wasn't human and that was a problem. So I figured, 'What I need is a girl.' But it turned out the girl *was* human and *that* was a problem. So I wound up working at GM to pay off the car and the girl."

And he introduced me to his pregnant wife, of whom he seemed much fonder than it sounded.

The young couple had no complaints about the pay at GM. Still, Duane planned to quit after his wife had the baby. "I'm staying so we can use the hospital plan." After that? "Maybe we'll go live on the land." If that didn't pan out, he'd look for a job where he'd get to do something "worthwhile."

To Duane worthwhile work didn't mean launching a space shuttle or curing cancer. It meant getting to see something he'd accomplished like fixing the coffeehouse record player, as opposed to performing his assigned snaps, twists, and squirts on cars that moved past him every thirty-six seconds.

He also wanted to escape the military atmosphere of the auto plant. "It's just like the army," he told me. "They even use the same words, like 'direct order.' Supposedly, you have a contract, so there's some things they just can't make you do. Except if the foreman gives you a direct order, you do it or you're out."

So despite the high pay, Duane and his friends talked about moving on. This wasn't just a pipe dream. In the early 1970s there was enough work around that if a friend moved to Atlanta or there was a band you liked in Cincinnati, you could hitchhike there and find a job in a day or two that would cover your rent and food.

That made it hard to run a business of course. The GM management echoed many other U.S. employers when it complained about Monday/Friday absenteeism and high turnover among young workers. At just about that time U.S. manufacturers began feeling competition from German and Japanese products, and for the first time in decades they saw a slight dip in profit rates. In retrospect I wonder if this wasn't the historic moment when many companies determined to do something about their labor problem.

But neither Duane nor I had any premonition of the outsourcing and off-shoring soon to come. For us it was a time when jobs abounded and Americans talked not about finding work but about humanizing it.

SCENE III

In the 1980s I spoke at a university in Michigan and spotted Duane in the audience. When the talk ended, I asked him to come out with us—me and the professors who'd invited me there. But Duane had to collect his children from their schools and drop them with the sitter in time to get himself to his 4:00 p.m. shift. His wife would pick them up when her day shift ended an hour later.

"Complicated logistics," I said.

"It's a tighter maneuver than my company in Nam ever pulled off," he quipped. But he and his family pulled it off every day.

In the minutes we had, Duane told me that he no longer worked in auto. "Too many layoffs." In order to "keep ahead of it," he'd become a machinist. And to keep ahead of that, he'd upgraded his skill to the point where "I program the machines that program the other machinists." His shrug said, "What are you gonna do?"

At that time, computers were being introduced into machine shops in a way that took the planning away from the operators at their benches and centralized it in the office or planning department. Duane was helping to fine-tune the automation that would reduce many of his skilled co-workers to machine tenders. He understood that he was "keeping ahead of it" by rendering other men cheaper and more replaceable. Hence his apologetic shrug.

His wife apparently hadn't managed to keep ahead of computer automation. She processed data at an insurance company and came home most evenings with a headache from staring into the era's immobile, blinking CRT screens.

"Office work is getting to be worse than those factories you wrote about," Duane told me. "By the way, I liked the book." He meant my book *All the Livelong Day*, with a chapter on Lordstown in which he appears.

A Phone Call

In the summer of 2008 a man called to say that he and his sisters were contacting names in their father's address book to let them know that he had passed away.

Duane died suddenly in Arizona, where he'd moved a few years earlier to work in a specialized shop that had something to do with industrial lasers. (He "kept ahead of it" till the end, it seems.) The funeral was scheduled for Saturday, and there was plenty of room for out-of-town guests. "Dad built these beautiful built-in sleeping spaces," his son told me.

Duane's children (the kids who'd been shuttled between shifts with such split-second timing) were trying to figure out how to keep the house in the family instead of selling it to a stranger who might not appreciate their father's craftsmanship. But all of that was still "up in the air."

I didn't go to the funeral, but I did at least manage to send a timely note of condolence.

Lehman Brothers collapsed two months later, and I began interviewing people who'd lost jobs, homes, or savings in the Great Recession for this book. It took me two years of talking to recession victims to see how Duane's pre-crash history, the parts I'd been privy to, explained the crisis that hit the rest of us after he died.

Once I realized that Duane and his family belonged in a history of the Great Recession, I tracked his son down. He told me that his sisters, both living in Michigan, had toyed with the idea of moving to Arizona, maybe together, though one was married and the other wasn't. They'd even begun to explore the employment situation out there. (One of Duane's daughters is a medical receptionist and the other a delivery truck driver.)

Then came the crash, and who would give up a steady job? Unfortunately, while they'd waited, house values dropped to the point that even if they managed to sell Duane's house at its post-crash price, they'd still owe the bank over $200,000. The house, with all Duane's beautiful built-ins, was now "underwater."

Since their mother was by then off the scene and their father had left no other significant inheritance beyond a $15,000 death benefit and a $6,000 credit card debt, his children couldn't afford to keep paying the mortgage. So, on the advice of a lawyer, they mailed the keys to the bank and walked away.

"Dad would make some joke," his son said. " 'When I was alive, I once stopped you from *running* away from home, but I taught you to *walk* away from a home after I was dead.' Something like that. Only he'd make it come out funny."

There is probably some way to make it come out funny, but I can't work out the wording either.

This is not to say that Duane led a deprived or worthless life. His estate may have fallen victim to the recession, but he himself worked fairly steadily at increasingly skilled and, let's hope, "worthwhile" jobs. He raised three children who get along with one another and admire their father. And he seems to have retained his self-aware but not self-deprecating humor to the end.

On the other hand: here's a workingman, part of a two-income family, who kept ahead of off-shoring, kept ahead of automation, worked for four decades, and died with no savings, negative equity in his house, and a $6,000 credit card debt.

Apropos of that credit card, Duane's son insisted on telling me that his dad derided "consumerism" to the end. While he was growing up, the family never bought a big-screen TV, a new car, or the season's must-have sneakers on credit. Most of the $6,000 debt, he thought, was left from Duane's last move from Illinois to Arizona, a career investment, one might call it, that he'd been paying down.

All of this suggests to me that while his skills went up, Duane's real wages stayed level or may even have gone down over his lifetime. But down is an un-American direction.

From 1820 to 1970, real hourly wages in America rose every decade—even over the course of the 1930s. That extraordinary century and a half (probably unique in history) ended in the 1970s. From then till now—in other words, throughout the course of Duane's working life—U.S. hourly wages stagnated or declined.*

Duane seems to fall into the high end—the stagnant end, that is—of that income statistic. During the years when so much work was moved abroad and so much industrial skill was transferred from human to computer, Duane was one of the foresighted or fortunate Americans who managed to "keep ahead of it."

Why, then, do I say that his life predicted the Great Recession?

Over the decades during which Duane's earnings were close to flat and his less skilled or less fortunate colleagues lost ground, U.S. productivity rose immensely. To put that statistically, between 1971 and 2007, U.S. productivity increased by 99 percent; that is, it nearly doubled. Over those same years hourly wages rose by 4 percent. (That's not 4 percent a year; it's 4 percent over thirty-six years.) In other words, the average worker's productivity rose

---

* These figures come from Professor Richard D. Wolff, who made this point in his monthly lecture series, Update on the State of Global Capitalism, delivered at the Brecht Forum in New York City. The lectures can be viewed online at brechtforum.org.

twenty-five times more than his pay.* People like Duane and his computerized white-collar wife produced more and more per hour even as their wages stayed constant or declined.

But the United States is a consumer economy. Duane used that word "consumer" to chide his children's craving for the in thing. But to economists "consumer economy" is a neutral term to describe a society that sells most of what it produces internally. In the United States we sell 70 percent of the goods and services we make to each other. But if the majority of Americans was earning less and producing more, who was going to buy all the stuff?

When Henry Ford raised assembly line wages to a fabulous $5 a day in 1914, he explained that his company couldn't grow unless Americans earned enough to buy the cars it made. When the companies Duane worked for began to cut wages, they reasoned that instead of *paying* their workers enough to buy stuff, they could *lend* them the money. Or perhaps they didn't so much reason as fall into the practice of necessity.

When Duane worked for General Motors in the early 1970s, it was an automaker that had gotten into auto loans to promote

---

* These statistics were collected for me by Doug Henwood, editor of the *Left Business Observer*. Henwood adds, with his characteristic fairness, that if you count fringe benefits, which were pushed up primarily by the rising cost of medical insurance, then the average employer's full hourly labor bill went up by almost half (49 percent) between 1971 and 2007. While costly to employers, that money didn't go to workers in a form they could spend, nor did it generally increase their standards of living. So to be totally fair if inelegant, we might say that between 1971 and 2007 productivity gains were twenty-five times hourly wage gains and two times wage-plus-benefits gains. Either figure is a radical break from the historic U.S. tradition of far more evenly shared productivity gains.

sales of its own products. By the time Duane died, General Motors Acceptance Corporation was not only an auto lender but the fourth-largest home mortgage lender in America. The TARP program bailed it out of massive subprime mortgage losses.

Similarly, that other industrial icon, General Electric, established its lending arm, GE Capital, to help midsized manufacturers finance their purchases of GE generators. But as real wages fell and real sales growth slowed, it too morphed into a financial firm. By 2007, the year before the crash, GE Capital contributed half of GE's profits.

Corporations that didn't become banks themselves deposited their profits in outside banks or returned them to shareholders who did the same. Thus Main Street money became Wall Street money. To put it another way, our economy became financialized. But what were financial institutions doing with all the money that was accumulating in fewer and fewer hands?

In my book *Money Makes the World Go Around*, I tried tracing my own bank deposit as it flowed out into the global economy in the mid-1990s. Most of my money, I discovered, coursed round and round through closed circuits for the trading of currencies, securities, and more abstract derivatives. The little that seeped out into what bankers call the "real sector" might be used to buy things like third-world water and power systems (without making any material improvements in them). A lot of the rest was lent to companies, countries, and private citizens who seemed to have no expanding business or rising income with which to pay that money back.

You couldn't miss the Ponzi-ish smell. If I don't have $10 this year and my wages aren't going up, how will I have $15 next year to pay you back with interest? Take out more loans? By the late 1990s it was obvious to anyone but a central banker that this couldn't go on much longer.

If it sounds as if I'm flaunting my own economic prescience, let me state for the record that while I shook my head over student loans, leveraged buyouts, dot-com stocks, and credit card debt, I did *not* predict that the ultimate Ponzi scheme of the era would involve selling, securitizing, and betting against home loans made to Americans who couldn't afford houses.

All I knew was that the United States is a consumer economy. But instead of sharing the productivity growth of the last forty years with our consumers, we divided it so unequally that most of the new wealth went to 1 percent, leaving the other 99 percent, including Duane, too poor to keep buying what they produce. Eventually, it caught up with us.

Yet once I started talking to victims of the Great Recession, I noticed something odd. "Poor" Americans are surprisingly rich. The breadlines of 1929 have been staved off by unemployment insurance. The two-income family, though it may have been a response to declining wages, is another form of unemployment insurance. Most people who are out of work not only eat but stop for take-out coffee. Not a single one of the long-term unemployed you're about to meet carried a thermos.

I'm aware, of course, that over 15 percent of the U.S. population lives below the official poverty line and that a sizable number face what we now call food insecurity. But I began this study by contacting people who had lost a job, a home, or savings in the Great Recession. That means they had one or more of those "middle-class" accoutrements to begin with.

A couple of people I talked with began to suspect, in the very course of our conversations, that they may "recover" from the recession by landing in a different socioeconomic class. Some have distressing ways of coping with their insecurity. But you'll also meet people with a real talent for snatching moments of pleasure and creating reassuring small routines, even when they can't be sure of larger patterns like where they'll work the next month or, in a couple of cases, where they'll sleep the next night.

As I talked with people who've lost jobs, homes, and savings, I couldn't help wondering what shape they and the country will be in after we fully emerge from the downturn. I think there are enough clues in their individual histories for us to make some good guesses by the time we're finished.

In the meantime, I've tried to leave these recession vignettes open-ended enough for you to glimpse a lot that's contradictory or irrelevant to my economic notions. That may be the best reason to travel along with me and see how specific, unique Americans cope with the Great Recession.

I: OUR JOBS

Chapter One

THE PINK SLIP CLUB

April 2009

Did you ever wonder how Jerry, George, Elaine, and Kramer of *Seinfeld* manage to pay Manhattan rents with those flaky jobs of theirs?

I met a group of four single New Yorkers who had worked at unglamorous office jobs and devoted their incomes—one earned $48,000 a year, one earned $52,000, and I'm guessing that the others earned around the same (they didn't say)—to maintaining themselves, supporting their church, and experiencing the city.

Even before they lost their jobs, the four friends were constantly in and out of Geraldine's, or Gerri's, condominium near Lincoln Center. When Gerri mentioned to the congregation that she was now unemployed, her friend Elaine, who'd already been out of work for two months, said, "We ought to start a Pink Slip Club."

The idea was to keep each other's spirits up and to enjoy inexpensive outings around the city. "We might as well make something positive out of having free time during the day—while it lasts," Elaine had said optimistically.

In the first couple of weeks they'd gone to a museum and to

an afternoon concert, and Elaine had come over to Gerri's to play Scrabble.

"Let's do it again," Gerri said.

"It was fun," Elaine agreed. "But it felt strange in the middle of the day."

Our Elaine is tall, blond, and more overtly glamorous than her *Seinfeld* namesake. Like *Seinfeld*'s Elaine, she can be a bit prickly, but that's only when she senses disapproval or misunderstanding of her intentions. And unlike *Seinfeld*'s Elaine, she's spontaneously generous. The job she lost involved processing accounts payable for a broadcasting conglomerate.

Gerri is short, dark, and quiet. When she speaks, it's often to encourage others to express what they mean more fully or to point out the basic agreement that underlies seeming differences. I could tell how good she makes others feel by the way the doorman smiled when I asked for her and how he sang into the intercom, "Gerri, you have company." For over twenty years Gerri had worked as an insurance adjuster at an office a short walk from her apartment.

Gerri and Elaine are suitable names for the two women, but it would raise constant misleading mental images to call the men George and Kramer. So I'm going to call them Kevin and Feldman from the *Seinfeld* episode where Elaine starts hanging out with three alternate buddies who turn out to be just too nice for her. It won't throw you far off if you think of the Pink Slip men as agreeable *Seinfeld* avatars.

Kevin is slim, well-groomed, and precise. He frequently restates what the others say with just a small editorial tweak. Perhaps that's because I'm there and he wants to make sure that the historical record is correct. But it may also be because Kevin was an editor at a trade journal. Despite the tendency to edit his friends, he's attentive to them in matters like holding doors, locating things they've carelessly set down, collecting information they can use, offering refreshments around, and similar thoughtfulness.

Feldman, the second Pink Slip Club male, is a solidly built guy who practices kung fu, rides a motorcycle, plays in a drumming circle, and has a tendency to take the last two cookies on the plate. (But he'll put one back if he notices.) Feldman did graphics—text layout—at a textbook company.

Before we met, Gerri had told me on the phone about the day she lost her job. "I was paralyzed. Or not paralyzed but jelly, because somehow I could move. I got my stuff together like a zombie. Six other people in our department got laid off that day, so I know it wasn't me. But it's like a divorce. You see your co-workers as much as your family. More, because the whole time in the office you're pretty much awake; a big part of the time at home you're asleep."

A colleague from another department called to ask Gerri out for dinner that evening. "She does that every time one of her friends gets laid off." I have since met the woman, and she reports that Gerri appeared to move through the rest of the day with her usual quiet purposefulness. But that's not how it felt to the victim.

"For the next three days I had migraine headaches. Then I got a cold. It had to be from the stress. I'm *slow*ly pulling out of it. I'm getting my résumé together."

Our phone conversation took place less than two weeks after the blow. Despite apologies that she was still sleepwalking, Gerri e-mailed her Pink Slip Club comrades and got back to me with a meeting date for early the next week. By the time I met her in person, a plan of action was taking shape.

Gerri is active in a national civic organization whose name you'd almost certainly recognize. The New York chapter is large enough to have a local president paid $50,000. That's only a couple of thousand less than Gerri's salary as an insurance adjuster, and Gerri had thought about pursuing it in the past. But despite encouragement from other members of the board of directors, she'd always hesitated to quit a permanent job for one that would only last one or two years. Besides, the local presidency isn't available for the asking; you have to run. But now, she says, "I'm unemployed, I might as well go for it. Maybe the Goddess is telling me this happened to me for a reason." (The four Pink Slip Club members happen to be Wiccans and their congregation a coven. Hence, the "Goddess.")

We had a few minutes to talk about the idea before the others arrived.

Elaine came to Gerri's place straight from visiting a friend in Queens who'd lost her job in the same round of cuts at the broadcasting company.

"We worked in different buildings, so first we told each other our stories, then we had lunch in this wonderful Greek restaurant. It was crowded, but from the talk I heard, nobody was having a business lunch. I wondered, what do all these people do? It's like they're on a holiday in Florida. My friend was going to have a pedicure afterward. 'Bring a book, just read and sit there and have a pedicure.' She said we'll do that together next time I go out there. Just relax and have a pedicure."

"You just have to treat yourself every now and then when you're on unemployment," Gerri said approvingly.

"And she's going to Yellowstone next week. She's always wanted to go to Yellowstone."

I wrecked Elaine's mood by asking her to describe what happened on the day she was fired.

"The word is not 'fired'!"

"I'm sorry, I just meant . . ."

"Someone is fired when they do something bad. I was laid off because they found a computer program to do the invoicing."

I apologized, stammering that to me a layoff meant something temporary, like a seasonal layoff at a factory. If they weren't going to call you back, then "layoff" was a euphemism.

Feldman explained the term's functional significance for him. " 'Laid off' means you can still collect your severance and unemployment. You didn't get fired for cause."

Though still annoyed, Elaine brought herself back to that day. "We got an e-mail that morning from the head of the whole company saying there were going to be some changes and layoffs. As soon as I finished reading that e-mail, we got one from the head of X [one of their big stations] saying, 'Oh, it's hard to say good-bye to people.' And I thought, 'Oh, shut up!' Then my phone rang, and the division head's assistant said, 'Les wants to see you in the office in five minutes.' And I knew what it was.

"When I got to his office, he was just getting there, and I said, 'Oh, am I the first?' And he said, 'You know it's not performance, Elaine.' He was just being so condescending.

"I said, 'I know it's not performance. I don't need to hear it.'"

Les asked Elaine to stay on for several weeks because the new computer system wasn't up yet. "'Your final day will be February 27 . . . We know you'll be professional to the very . . .'

"I said, 'I'll just go and talk to HR.' I didn't let him finish."

In HR, Elaine saw the woman assigned to present each person's severance package and to make sure that everyone eventually signed a release freeing the company from any further obligation. "She said if I wanted to, I could take the rest of the day off.

"I said, 'I can't do that! This is the day we're closing the month and the year for payrolls. [It was the beginning of December.] I have work to do!' Later I told her, 'I'll take tomorrow and Friday off.' Friday would count as one of my entitled free days, so it wouldn't come out of my severance package.

"Of course I was going to remain professional till the end. There are people I worked with who need answers from me to get their jobs done. That's what I was there for. It's not their fault." Elaine was proud that throughout nine years of mergers, buyouts, and other corporate discombobulations, she had kept those paychecks coming to the network's celebrities, behind-the-camera employees, and vendors.

Elaine continued the story to the final moments of her final day when someone from human resources came down with her severance agreement.

"She said, 'Do you want to sign it right here?' I said no." (Elaine knew that she had forty-five days to get the agreement back to the company and had already hired a lawyer to look at it.)

"I asked, 'Do I have to go see anybody else before I leave?' She said, 'Nobody's going to walk you out.' So I went up to the shredder, I took my ID, I put it in the shredder, and then I walked out the door. It was a fairly nice day out. That night I went to the ballet and had a nice time."

Isolated details from the moment of being fired (or laid off) have a way of becoming embedded in our minds. (Some wounded soldiers remember the bullet approaching in agonizing slow motion.) Fortunately, most of us soon encapsulate or neutralize the painful details by arranging them into a story that protects our dignity.

Elaine's story shows her to be loyal to her colleagues and to her professional duties while treating the corporate types with the caustic but dignified disdain they deserved. As an added fillip, she enjoyed herself at the ballet that night. Not only that, but "the first day I wasn't working it was a really big snowstorm and I was just delighted that I didn't have to go anywhere." I guess we know whose side the gods are on.

Kevin's integrity had come into play years before his actual layoff from a finance-related professional organization, and that's where he started his account when I asked what happened.

"With the Sarbanes-Oxley Act of 2002, our members had a lot to learn and relearn. At that point the editor in chief [Kevin worked on the organization's journal], who started around the same time that I did, realized that we could not only provide information on the new rules to our members; we could become the voice of our industry speaking to the regulators and standard setters in Washington, D.C. He was very much a visionary."

According to Kevin, the publication did, indeed, gain stature. But eventually the editor moved on. "It took me a while to realize that the new editor was not a visionary. The only question for her was how to maintain the status quo. So I found another position within the organization. But when the economic downturn came, several people were let go. I had kind of lost respect for the organization on account of the magazine becoming so status quo. I have no regrets really."

In Kevin's story, professional integrity dictated that he transfer from a secure position to one where he had insufficient seniority. This is as close as he got to describing the painful moment to me. But he liked to talk about the adventuresome decade before.

Ten years earlier Kevin had sold his house in Chicago, moved to New York without a job, and bought an apartment on Christopher Street. "I remade myself," he said.

In New York he volunteered on weekends for a charity venture that raises considerable money for people with AIDS and for the homeless. Now he'd added a weekday shift. "I made a conscious decision to volunteer more because it would give me more of a structure and sense of purpose.

"I'm economical." (Kevin's friends confirmed that with fond laughs.) "I'm collecting unemployment. I probably have enough savings to survive until I start collecting Social Security. So I don't have the urgency that Feldman has. But in some ways I wish I did because . . . the older I get the harder it's going to be to find another job. I almost wouldn't mind feeling a little more anxious. My biggest fear is that this will turn into, you know, the beginning of my retirement. I don't want that." Kevin is fifty-four.

I hadn't yet asked these four unemployed New Yorkers how they were supporting themselves. But it didn't seem to be an immediate concern to anyone except Feldman.

When he got out of college, Feldman had a girlfriend who acted as a subcontractor, hiring freelancers to do graphics for textbooks and magazines. As a recent and unemployed grad, Feldman hung around her apartment and noticed that she could never find enough reliable, skilled hands. He decided that he would master the craft. He even paid her for a few lessons on the most advanced programs.

Feldman soon had all the work he needed. In fact, his first job was a marathon of twelve-hour shifts, seven days a week. "I went from earning nothing to making thirty grand in three months. It's the most I ever earned in that industry." All Feldman wanted was enough work to support himself, his rent-stabilized apartment in Inwood in northern Manhattan, and his motorcycle and his hobbies.

Over the years jobs got a bit scarcer, and Feldman sometimes had to take $25 an hour instead of $30. The more distressing development was that contractors took to paying freelancers forty-five, sixty, or even ninety days after the work was delivered. If they went out of business or if a client defaulted (and those things seemed to be happening more and more often), they "stiffed the guy at the bottom of the totem pole," Feldman said.

"Yes, there's a lot of freelancers getting stiffed," Kevin confirmed.

"Sorry, our client didn't pay us, so we can't pay you—boo-hoo-hoo," Feldman japed. "One time it made me so angry that I went up to the office, and I didn't physically threaten the guy in charge, but I did intimidate. And of all the people who got paid, I wound up getting paid first."

After thirteen years as a freelancer, "I couldn't take the insecurity anymore," Feldman confessed.

It seemed to me that just as he had once slipped casually into freelancing, so Feldman had slipped casually into adulthood. Financial insecurity was more stressful to him in his late thirties than it had been in his mid-twenties. But Feldman presented it less in terms of personal evolution and more in terms of changing business practices. "In order to play as a freelancer these days, you have to have a five- to six-thousand-dollar stake. You need a prudent reserve of like three months."

It took him six months to find the staff job that he'd held for two and a half years before the recession started. Then the textbook company fired twenty people. The way Feldman describes the day, his immediate response had been hard and cool.

"First they sent us in in groups, like cattle going to the slaughter. Then they brought us in one by one to explain the terms of the severance. My boss's boss and someone higher than her, they're smiling, saying how nice we're going to treat you, and I'm sitting there like daggers coming out of my eyes.

"Some people just got the hell out of there, like they were in shock. But I stayed because I had stuff of my own on the computer that wasn't backed up."

"At least they didn't cut off your access," I said. I told him about a group of engineers who'd been brought to a hotel, ostensibly for a meeting, only to be told that all computer codes were being changed and that they would all be accompanied while they cleaned out their desks.

"Yeah, we had a guy, had a breakdown in the office. They said, 'Okay, you're being escorted off.' But with this mass layoff they said, 'You'll have till two o'clock to get your stuff together.' Since it started about ten, eleven in the morning, it gave me like three hours to back up my files and wipe every trace of myself off that computer."

"You weren't paralyzed like I would be," I said.

"Not then and there. But when I got home, I was a basket case. Then I went into panic mode. I said I better redo my résumé before the weekend. And I did. But there were a couple of openings I could have applied for the next day—before everyone else got into the mad rush of the job hunt. One of them went to someone I worked with who may have already worked for that company on a free-lance basis, so she may have had the job locked up. But I don't know what would have happened if I applied."

In normal times, starting your job hunt a day or a week later can change your fate in that unknowable way that crossing a street at a certain moment puts you on the path to encounter the love of your life. Cross a moment later, and you'll meet another love and have a different life. But that's not how fate worked during the Great Recession.

"That was in November [2008], and this is February [2009]," Feldman reminded us. "I haven't come across any other staff positions since those two. Actually, one of them was a temp job. But it could have been ongoing, and it was thirty bucks an hour. I would like to have got that. I would like to have at least applied so I don't have this what-if thing now."

If there were no steady jobs, what about one-night stands? I wondered. Even temp work was hard to find, Feldman said. Besides, he had to be careful about that. If he worked more than two days, he'd lose all his unemployment money for that week, yet he couldn't expect to receive his freelance pay for at least forty-five days. "That's one and a half months. Who can survive?"

"So you're living on unemployment?"

"Yes. The regular unemployment is twenty-six weeks, but now, because of the economy, they've added thirty-three weeks, so it's like over a year."

"And you plan to go on collecting for the full year?"

"Not if I have anything to say about it. I'm looking for work every day. On what unemployment pays, I come out a couple of hundred bucks a month short. And I've only got $1,600 of the severance left."

"And when that's gone?" I asked.

He couldn't stop eating or paying the landlord. The only significant expense Feldman could think of cutting was the insurance on his motorcycle. Even as we spoke, the Suzuki 1250 was waiting faithfully downstairs. The idea of putting it in storage was almost unbearable. He just had to find a job.

"I looked yesterday but not this morning. I use twenty, thirty Web sites. Most I found on my own. When you go to unemployment, they actually have a list of Web sites they give you. Some are really crappy, but some are decent."

"And some are better for certain types of jobs than others," Kevin explained to me.

"I use three key words," Feldman said. "I'll do 'production artist,' 'Quark,' and 'art and design' because those are the primary things that will bring me work."

"Have you tried Mediabistro.com?" Kevin asked.

"Yeah, I go there. I pretty much have all the bases covered. My problem is the companies out there are combining jobs. They say, 'Oh, well, since this is such an economic crisis, we can get the cream of the crop. So let's not just hire production artists; let's hire somebody who has a design degree, is a production artist, and does HTML, CSS, Java . . . They want designer and production in one. Not just production."

Gerri showed me the church's fund-raising calendar that Feldman designs, lays out, and does everything else on. It was good-looking. His friends even thought he might try making it a commercial venture. He seemed to have a variety of graphics skills.

"I have the technical skills, but they want somebody who also has a four-year degree in design, which I don't have."

"Have you thought about enrolling toward a degree while you're unemployed?" I asked.

"I don't know how I could afford it. For a four-year degree, who'd cover me financially?"

Kevin offered encouragement. "It wouldn't take you four years, because you already have a background. Also, there might be some kind of certificate."

"But are they going to hire someone with a certificate compared to someone with a degree?" Feldman said, defending his unmarketability.

"But you have experience that an entry-level person does not and . . ."

Not to be consoled, Feldman told us about a friend who had both a degree and design awards but still couldn't find a job.

"How old is he?" Kevin asked. "Mid- to late forties? Older people face different challenges." Kevin said that companies wanted to hire recent grads rather than people in their fifties.

"I don't think they're looking to hire somebody fresh out of school," Feldman contradicted Kevin. "I just think they're looking for people who have more skills."

Neither of the two seemed willing to grant the other the comfort of believing that his situation was hopeless.

"So what will you do if your severance money runs out before you find a job?" I asked.

"I would probably ask a friend to borrow money. But it probably won't come to that. And it will be friends with jobs," he assured the others.

Feldman got to his bottom line. "I have a motorcycle I have to protect and insure. So it's either get employed or get a wife real fast."

"A working wife," Gerri tossed in.

"She doesn't have to have a job," Feldman replied. "Two unemployments would cover things."

Just how desperate are these folks? Feldman had mentioned that his mother pays for his health insurance and that he had recently earned some money painting her apartment while she was wintering in Florida. I also know that he doesn't get along with his stepfather, who has the money in the family. From all of that I surmise that, horrible as it would feel, Feldman could count on some kind of contribution from his family if he were about to lose his apartment.

Elaine has an inheritance from an aunt. It came up when she complained about a snafu at the unemployment office because her investment manager labeled some investment income in a way that triggered alarm bells. From her telling of the story, she seems to have handled the unemployment office bureaucrats with the same caustic control she'd used on the flunkies who fired her. She'd straightened the matter out, and her benefits were restored.

I couldn't ask Elaine exactly how much money she had inherited, but she probably wasn't about to be pushed onto the street either. And Kevin had volunteered that he could survive till he started collecting Social Security.

Of the four, Gerri's finances seemed the most finite, dependent on her own earnings, that is.

She'd complained that the maintenance fees on her condominium had gone up by 30 percent since she bought the place. The obvious financial recourse for someone with such a desirable apartment was to take a roommate. But Gerri had already resorted to that after an earlier life crisis. "I love this apartment, and I wanted to keep it after I was divorced." So she already had a roommate for the past few years. (That explained the man who padded silently up the hallway, opened the refrigerator, and slipped back down the hallway a couple of times during our get-together.)

I know that Gerri's mother was a legal secretary who hadn't worked in twenty years and lives in special-care housing of some kind. Gerri hadn't told her mother about the divorce for almost three years. "She's bipolar, and she'd blow everything out of proportion. I tell my mother things on a need-to-know basis." Gerri had eventually mentioned her divorce to her mother as a way to explain why she didn't have money to give to her sister who was pursuing an acting career.

"But I had to tell her about the job right away because she used to call me at work every day. If I didn't say something, I'd come home and find ten phone calls."

I deduce, then, that Gerri can't expect financial help from her immediate family nor inheritances from her extended family in Mexico. As a first-generation American, a first-generation college graduate, and the levelheaded one in the family, she'd be expected to give, not receive, the help.

Though she didn't have a middle-class family behind her, Gerri surely had more savings than Feldman. Through its 401(k) plan, her employer of twenty-one years had matched any investment she made up to 5 percent of her salary. "For my first two years there I had a real pension [a traditional, defined-benefit plan]. Then they switched to a 401(k). Mine was down $30,000 when I lost my job." On the advice of a friend in finance, she rolled over the 401(k) and bought an annuity after her layoff. "I felt at least I'll have *some-thing* that's guaranteed."

How large, then, are Gerri's savings? At the height of the financial crisis, the kinds of prudent, diversified portfolios that employer-selected brokerages offered investors like Gerri went down between 25 and 40 percent. Gerri had lost $30,000 at that point. So she probably had somewhere between $75,000 and $120,000 of pre-tax savings to invest in that annuity.

When I asked directly how she's holding up, she told me, "Maintenance [on the condo] is up to fourteen hundred something, and then there's the mortgage. When you need $2,000 a month just to pay for housing, $400 [her weekly unemployment benefit] doesn't go that far. I better get into find-a-job mode."

When it came to lifestyle changes, "I never made that much, and I don't spend that much. I wear sweatshirts and jeans in the winter, T-shirts and jeans in the summer. But I can get dressed up if I have to," she assured me. "I went to a show once or twice a year; I'll cut that. I always wanted to try facials, and I finally bought six of them, prepaid, right before. So I'll use them up."

"It's all relative," Gerri philosophized. "If you're used to going to Per Se [a bizarrely expensive Manhattan restaurant] once a week and spending four, five hundred dollars for dinner, having to go across the street to Josephina and only spending $200 is the same thing as me not being able to go to a concert."

The Pink Slippers certainly worried about their finances and compared notes on practical matters. Elaine, for instance, was taking all the medical tests she could—"mammogram, bone density"— while she still had free time and the company health coverage. "But you can only do a couple of tests a week. I had a colonoscopy last Friday and a CAT scan the Friday before."

We all had something to say about that disgusting colonoscopy prep. But no one knew how to evaluate a more serious argument against taking all the medical tests you can. What if they find something? Would that mean you had put a preexisting condition on your medical chart just as the company coverage expired and you had to find a policy on your own?

Feldman reminded us that "under some part of the stimulus, the government covers part of your COBRA payments. That's only for nine months; I have six left."

"I really hope I'm not fooling around looking for a job by then," Elaine said.

Though the four friends were thinking about some lifestyle adjustments, no one was scrimping on food or taking coffee with them in a thermos. As Gerri pointed out, "It's all relative."

Elaine summed up her mood by quoting John Lennon: "Time that you enjoy wasting is not wasted."

Gerri quoted Eleanor Roosevelt: "A woman is like a tea bag. You never know how strong she is until she gets into hot water."

Feldman said he was depressed despite many evening activities. But he had been mildly depressed before—"chronic dysthymia," he called it. His immediate psychological need was to fill that "nine-to-five hole."

Before we split up, the friends firmed up some plans. Elaine and Feldman arranged a time to rehearse a scene. "We're taking an acting class. We have to learn to play off each other," Feldman explained.

He also proposed a movie day. "*Terminator 4* is coming out in a week." He'd check with a friend who could sometimes get them invited to screenings. "She's press," he told me.

Finally, they went over their responsibilities for upcoming church events and invited me to a public ceremony on May 1.

"It's called Beltane," Kevin explained. "It's to welcome the spring."

"It's all right to come just out of curiosity," Gerri assured me.

"Bring fifteen feet of colored ribbon," Feldman said.

"Huh?"

"Maypole ribbon."

"Wow, I never did a real maypole."

Spring Ritual 2009

The Beltane ceremony was held in Central Park, and I didn't need to bring my own maypole ribbon.

A member set up a traditional pole still displaying the ribbons that had been woven by dancers the preceding spring. Another member taught us—there were about seventy-five attendees—to dance around it with joy sufficiently tempered that we crossed over and under leaving more neatly woven ribbon on the pole. I also learned how to braid flower garlands that stay together. Elaine's wreath fit with real flair and matched her flower-print skirt.

"Beltane" is Gaelic for the month of May and for this festival. The rite has to do with bringing the sheep back to pasture. The heart of the ceremony as practiced in Central Park consisted in calling up individual gods and goddesses of antiquity and the Middle Ages. As we faced outward in a circle, I wondered what the people next to me actually believed about the divinities they welcomed. When I read *The Iliad* and *The Odyssey*, I take those talks with Athena literally. I also take the Nativity story literally when I attend midnight Mass.

Feldman, who led part of the ceremony as a bare-chested woodland spirit, said that his religion affords him a way to communicate with the male and female forces of the universe. Kevin, a Catholic, had found his way to paganism while he still lived in Chicago. He feels that he's calling to the divine power or spirit that resides in everything in creation. I wondered if Gerri (in her usual sweatshirt, jeans, and baseball cap) was consulting Astarte about the run for chapter president.

It was a beautiful spring day, and that may have influenced everyone's mood. All four of the Pink Slip Club members were still jobless, as were others among the participants I heard. But I don't think anyone strolling past us would have detected any recessionary pall over the spring ceremony.

September 2010

Sixteen months after I first met the group, Gerri organized a second Pink Slip get-together for my benefit. By that time she had run for the New York chapter presidency and lost. Her roommate had moved in with his girlfriend. This visit a young woman slipped down the hallway and out the front door.

"She's the only person I know of who quit a job," Gerri said. "She couldn't take her boss anymore."

"It must have been pretty bad to quit in this environment," Kevin remarked.

"Maybe her parents have money," Gerri speculated.

"Anything else new?" I asked. "I really could use to hear something hopeful." (By that time I'd been interviewing people outside New York where the recession hit harder and things had been worse to begin with.)

"I have my first job interview Wednesday," Gerri said. "It's with a New York liquidation bureau." We all laughed. "I know it sounds ironic," she acknowledged. "These people audit bankrupt insurance companies."

"Is that the one your friend saw on their Web site?" Kevin asked.

"Yeah," Gerri answered. A friend had spotted the quasi-public job listing while researching a mystery novel. "I applied four months ago. I was asleep when they called, and I said, 'Liquidators? I don't owe anybody any money.' Then it clicked. It took them all that time to get back to me—well, it's a government agency."

"You applied online?" I asked.

"Everything is online now. I have yet to see an actual person. Nobody wants to talk to anybody."

"But these people want to talk to you!" I said. The job involved estimating pending claims obligations of faltering or defunct insurers, and Gerri had been an insurance adjuster handling just such claims. Key words on her résumé must have rung dozens of electronic bells. "It sounds like a perfect match."

"And it's a government agency," Kevin said, adding his enthusiasm.

"Yes, good benefits." Gerri allowed herself a moment of optimism. "The only place you could get a real pension these days."

"Just about," Kevin said. "Yeah."

My superstitious fear of the evil eye dictated that we drop the subject. The only other member with job action to talk about was Elaine. She'd even had one and a half days of paid work.

"In July somebody called me from an agency and said, 'Hi, I saw your résumé on Monster.' He said, 'Our agency has a client. I'd like you to come in and talk to a colleague who'll be your friend on the inside.' I filled out a long form online, then went there and finished up on their computer." Someone named Mark told Elaine about a job involving accounts payable and took her payroll information.

"Then he didn't get back to me, and I said, 'Okay, I'm not surprised.' Then all of a sudden he called. He said, 'Hi, this is Mark.' I said, 'Who?' He said, 'Ah, how soon they forget.' This time he said, 'I have something lined up with an advertising company, and I want to send you the job description.'"

Several potential permanent jobs later, "Mark called and asked, 'Are you interested in doing some temping?' I said, 'Why, of course.' He said they needed some people to work on problem invoices downtown at M—— [another company whose name you'd know].

"I said, 'Great, I always have fun getting lost way down there. And by the way, what happened to L—— [the last full-time job Elaine was told she was up for]?' He said, 'Oh, they passed.' Then he said, 'This one is business casual, and it will last two weeks.' I had just bought some nice corporate-looking clothes, so fine. He sent four of us women up there on Friday."

The four temps had a longish wait before they met the woman they were supposed to report to. "She was very, I don't know, standoffish. So was the woman who was supposed to be giving us the work. The regular workers were very quiet, almost like robots. The girl who was supposed to help me with something, I complimented her on her bracelet, and it was almost like she was afraid to talk."

Elaine told of being moved from task to task—"Kathy has something for you to do on Excel" or "Okay, just continue with the purchase orders"—until quitting time.

"I stopped in her office to see if they had signed my time sheet, and she says, 'Oh, I won't need you girls on Monday.'"

"All four of you?" I asked.

"Yes, apparently, we all did such a good job. So we called Mark, and he said, 'Yeah, I heard.' So I went to pick up my check from the agency."

"How much did they pay you?" I asked.

"They paid me thirteen an hour. I think they paid the others less because one of the women said to me, 'I'm going to check with my agency; this is only eleven an hour.'"

I assumed that the experience had been frustrating. So I was surprised when Elaine said, "You know it was nice to be sitting in an office. To know that I still know how to walk into an office and sit down and turn on the computer. It was nice."

Elaine had had one other bit of work. "I have a friend who works for a doctor, and her colleague was going to be out for a funeral. I happened to have an interview with an agency in the afternoon, but I worked in the morning for several hours, and the doctor handed me the cash."

That was all the paid work that anyone had to report.

Feldman, who'd been the most depressed at the first get-together, skipped this one because his new girlfriend was visiting from out of town. She wasn't unemployed and she hadn't moved in with him, so she didn't bring the dowry of a second unemployment check that he'd wished for. Still, I assumed I'd find him a little less depressed when we got together.

But Gerri, Kevin, and Elaine, the members who'd thought of their Pink Slip Club as a way to make the most of a few free days or weeks, had grown more sober. By now they understood that this bout of unemployment was different from others they'd lived through.

Elaine remembered when a publishing conglomerate she'd worked for in past years went under. "I was talking to the woman in HR who handled benefits, and I said, 'You know what I'd like to do? I'd like to continue with accounts payable but in television.' I thought of that because we had a cable office in San Francisco. My boss didn't want anything to do with television, because it was totally different from accounts payable in publishing. So I was the liaison. Then I met all the girls from that S.F. office when they came to New York. They liked to tell me all the things they were seeing around the city.

"I only just mentioned that to the HR woman, and she said, 'A friend of mine just started working at HR at [the original channel of Elaine's now huge broadcasting network].' She said, 'When you're ready, give me your résumé, and I'll fax it to her.' I got the résumé ready in the office while I was still working; I sent it two days later, and I got the job. I loved that I didn't have to ask my ex-boss if I could use him as a reference. What I love about that job is the way it just came to me."

"I guess that's what you have to do now," I said. "Just talk, talk, talk to everyone."

"But who doesn't know ten people who are looking?" Kevin said.

"Exactly," Gerri said, seconding him.

Elaine is the one who least needed the advice to talk to people. "My dentist has my résumé; he wanted a hard copy. My chiropractor has my résumé. My friend Linda that I've known for a hundred years, she has it on her computer at work."

"I also had my last job fall in my lap," Gerri said. Her first job out of college was at an insurance company. After a brief stint her whole department was transferred to Florida. But living in New York is a great deal of what Gerri's life is about. Fortunately, she didn't have to consider the move. "My new job materialized before my last day on the old job."

"You were perfect for it," Kevin said.

"It was perfect timing," Gerri countered modestly. "I wasn't ever unemployed like for a minute."

"And now you have so much experience," I said. There couldn't be a better match for that insurance liquidating job, I was thinking. But I didn't want to jinx it by saying anything.

"But there are just so many people unemployed now," Gerri said.

"And we are not young." Kevin sounded his leitmotif.

Resentment rather than resignation was Elaine's fallback emotion. She had begun to notice how insensitive some of her friends are to the feelings of the jobless.

"Yesterday I went to stand out with, you know, my friend Rosalie, who does that kitten-rescue thing in front of the bank on Hudson Street. Well, she complained about her Pilates class, and I said that I liked Bonnie's class. She says"—here Elaine shifts into a gloriously callow whine—" 'Well, I can't take that because I work full-time.' "

"People like to complain," said Kevin. "I'm unemployed, but I still have my health."

"That little bit of work was such a nice break," Elaine said, shifting moods, "that I actually went out and bought myself another little jacket to wear with a black dress. I have several black blazers, but I wanted a colorful one that you could put over a black dress so you wouldn't have to wear a suit for interviews. A lot of people are doing that—a plain dress with a colorful jacket. I don't like suits at all."

Kevin and Elaine itemized Elaine's wardrobe until Kevin concluded, "So you're ready for short-term jobs and you're ready for interviews and you're ready for a full-time job when that comes around."

Elaine was indeed ready. I mentioned that I had interviewed a couple of wealthy people who panicked when the market dropped because they had to "dip into capital." Then they remembered those shares they got from Grandpa at the wedding, or some gold in a vault, or a brokerage account they thought they'd closed out . . .

"Those people should hire me as a personal assistant. I'd keep track of things," Elaine volunteered.

"I think a lot of people like that do have personal assistants," Gerri said.

"Handlers!" Elaine remembered the word. Many of the personalities she used to pay had handlers.

"I have two résumés," Gerri said. "One for straight insurance and one to get into the nonprofit world." Gerri's second résumé had been inspired by a listing for a six-month job as an "event planner" for an educational system. Gerri had done that sort of thing on a fairly large scale for the civic organization. So she'd translated her volunteer experience into résumé terms and applied.

"There are some people that say 'Change your résumé,'" Elaine declared. "I've already had people make sure my résumé looks like it should. The only way I could *change* it would be to totally lie and say I've done things that I haven't done. And that would be stupid."

It's possible that Elaine would have liked one of her friends to argue that changing one's résumé is not necessarily stupid. If I said it, she would surely have snapped at me. But with or without an enhanced résumé, Elaine is amazingly open to new careers.

"There's a little place on Seventy-second Street that will convert a vinyl record to a CD," she said. "They have a machine and there's an old man who sits there and they have some wild classical music that's playing so loud that I can hardly hear when I'm in there. I've come in and the old man is behind the desk and I'm standing there with a vinyl record in my hand and nobody asks, 'What do you want?' I'm not sure they even have a cash register.

"And I've often thought, maybe I'll walk in there someday and say, 'By the way, do you need anybody to help?' I like the place; I'm good at organizing. When I was working, a lot of people came to my desk because I was always happy to help them or to find someone who had that information. Everyone knew my name. When I called and said, 'Hi, this is Elaine,' they didn't have to ask my account number."

"So you think that store needs to get a little organized?" Kevin said.

"I don't know, maybe they like it that way. But just go in and if nothing else, ask people if they need help when they walk in. If they want to pay me a little something, that's okay, but just to go in and do something."

I asked Kevin if he was applying for jobs other than magazine editor. After all, that field had been declining even before the recession.

"Yes. Ideally, I would love to work for an arts organization, a museum. I know that I can live comfortably on less than I was making, and for something that I personally love and enjoy, it would be a good trade-off, as opposed to working on something that is just a paycheck. But I also know that the arts and that sector have taken a big hit too. The Metropolitan Museum with its huge budget has just laid off people. The big auction houses cut their staffs. So I'm not expecting what I was just describing for myself to happen quickly or easily. It would be a kind of dream job."

Gerri harked back to her dream job in events planning. "If I did it for six months, then I would have 'corporate experience.'"

"Did they ever get back to you?" Kevin asked.

"No, but they took four months to get back to me on this one," meaning the liquidator. "And once you're in the university system for six months, then . . ." She drifted off.

Elaine's far-ranging what-ifs made her all the more ready to seize the moment, and Kevin, as he mentioned, could live on his savings. But I began to worry about the way unemployment was incapacitating Gerri. Sixteen months earlier I'd said, offhandedly, that I'd like to talk to that office mate who took her out to dinner the day she lost her job. Gerri dialed her friend on the spot, made a useful introduction, and handed me the phone to firm up the appointment. Her special strain of "levelheadedness" consists in focusing clearly on the here and now and attending to the tasks necessary to move things one step forward. It wasn't a good sign for Gerri to be dwelling on a can't-do-anything-about-it matter. And besides, do people get back to you about a six-month job three months later?

Unlikely.

Autumn Equinox 2010

If a straight thinker like Gerri can't contemplate her prospects logically, maybe the prospects are too disturbing to face with mere logic.

Other people in her church must have been feeling the same

way, for the coven decided to add a "prosperity ritual" to the fall equinox ceremony. Kevin was to be the special facilitator. Though it was a closed ceremony, he invited a couple of sympathetic outsiders, including me and Feldman's new sweetheart, to the sunset event in Central Park.

We welcomed the four winds and other divine powers as usual. But the special honoree was the goddess Fortuna. First, though, we gave small gifts to appease her sister Nemesis so that she wouldn't counteract the benefits that Fortuna might grant.

Kevin had printed enlarged $100 bills for us to burn. He'd also dug up a money chant written by the very Benjamin Franklin whose face appears on those bills. The words came from a drinking song in a play Franklin co-wrote. A coven member created a tune, and we circled around the burning money pyre singing:

Then let us get money like bees lay in honey.
We'll build us new hives and we'll store each cell.
The sight of our treasure shall yield us great pleasure.
We'll count it and chink it and jingle it well.

So our multifaceted forefather didn't do *everything* well. After a few choruses the group spontaneously abandoned the Franklin chant and shifted into:

They say the best things in life are free
Well, you can tell that to the birds and bees

And they bellowed out versions of the song's various titles:

"I need money!" "I want money!" "Just give me money!"

Then a witch with a good voice sang:

Won't somebody buy me a Mercedes-Benz
My friends all have Jaguars, I must make amends.

Our individual communications with the goddess were private, of course. But toward the end of the ceremony everyone was given a chance to say what he would do with the wealth that Fortuna was going to bestow.

One woman said she'd build an animal shelter with a special section for small horses. Feldman was going to build a kung fu studio with an attached garage large enough to store all the motorcycles he'd buy. Gerri said she would bring her aunt from South Carolina to live in New York. Kevin told us that the Whitney Museum was planning to build an annex downtown. "Yes, right in our neighborhood," he said, nodding to me. "Well, there's going to be a Kevin M. Graham Room in that building." I wish I'd heard Elaine's prosperity plan, but she celebrated the equinox with another congregation.

And On It Goes

I like a story with a beginning, a middle, and an end. But between the spring and the fall rituals that should book-end this tale, the four members of the Pink Slip Club had morphed into "the long-term unemployed." They didn't retire, and they didn't find jobs. Their stories just dragged on.

I waited a decent couple of weeks after the ceremony to phone Gerri about her job interview with the liquidator. "The people in the office seemed to relate to each other in a good way," she reported. "Having nice people to work with is very important."

"So, um, what happened? Did they . . . ?"

"It took them four months to get to me," she said. "Maybe they'll get back to me."

I visited Feldman soon after his new girlfriend left town. She'd filled his freezer with casseroles so he knew where his next meal was coming from. As for work, "I had two weeks of employment since this began—around March last year. One week I made $600, the other week something less. It was like $50 more than my unemployment, that's after taxes."

His most immediate source of insecurity was his unemployment insurance.

"The pressure is high right now because in five weeks I'm going to become a 99er." That was the term for people who had used up their full ninety-nine weeks of extended unemployment benefits. Actually, it was ninety-three weeks in New York at that point because the state had a lower rate of unemployment than other parts of the country. Though this had started as a financial crisis, the rapid recovery on Wall Street brought the state's employment rate up. The unemployment extension was in the news because the 2010 congressional elections were coming up and there was a lot of acrimonious debate about stimuli like unemployment benefits versus deficit cutting through austerity.

"Right now there's a Democratic majority, and they're not doing anything about extending benefits," Feldman said. "In November there could be a Republican majority. That's just when the 99ers will be coming on in full swing because that's when people started getting laid off—November of two years ago.

"If this country doesn't get it together, they're going to storm the White House," Feldman predicted. "It will probably turn into anarchy, and then it will turn into martial law, and the government will be forced to, you know, use their own military against their own people. That would be sad because they have much better weapons than the people."

"It's funny, but I don't hear any rumblings of things like that," I said.

"Maybe they turn down the publicity on them. I don't even watch the news anymore. Most of the news is propaganda."

I felt certain that I would detect hints of a movement to storm the White House for unemployment benefits. The only thing then scheduled for D.C. was a march for moderation organized by two comedians. Admittedly, a group of loosely organized 99ers had demonstrated in front of the unemployment office on Varick Street in Manhattan in November 2010. They handed out a leaflet calling for unemployment benefits extensions and for a federal jobs program like those the Roosevelt administration created in the 1930s. As part of planned civil disobedience, they briefly blocked traffic. Four of about twenty demonstrators were arrested, handcuffed, and held about ninety minutes before being released. Their spokesmen urged other 99ers to take up the protest with or without civil disobedience. It got minimal media coverage, but eventually veterans of this and other barely noticed protests would heed an online call and come together at a square in downtown Manhattan to become the Occupy Wall Street movement. So maybe Feldman had a better sense of the national mood than I did.

"That Obama is not really as behind the people as he sounded like," Feldman said. "As far as I can tell, he's just another puppet in office."

A month later the Obama administration negotiated to continue extended unemployment benefits. It was done not in response to protests but as part of a legislative compromise that extended the Bush tax cuts. But the deal wouldn't mean any more money for Feldman. Earning the title 99er means you've graduated from the unemployment system. Feldman could only collect further benefits if he found a job, worked for the required period, lost the job, and qualified like any newly laid off worker. The tax-cut-for-benefits trade involved allocating money so that new people coming into the unemployment system could also get extensions beyond the normal twenty-six weeks if they qualified.

By the fall of 2010 there were fourteen million officially unemployed Americans—40 percent of them classified as the long-term unemployed. An additional ten million were working part-time but said they wanted full-time jobs. Fifteen million more had dropped out of the labor force since this recession began.

But bright, educated, unemployed people will surely drift into some kind of work eventually—won't they? Maybe Gerri will pick up freelance event-planning gigs through contacts at organizations where she's volunteered. Maybe Elaine will walk into a smart women's clothing store where she's shopped and ask for a job.

At the rate at which full-time staff jobs are being phased out, the older long-term unemployed of this recession probably have less than a fifty-fifty chance of finding permanent, full-time jobs.

But that's statistics. All any individual needs is *one* job.

Our Pink Slip Club protagonists are college graduates. They prepared themselves for the "symbolic manipulation" that was supposed to replace industrial work in our new knowledge economy, and they kept up their skills.

None of the four friends are world-beaters who start in the mail room and end up in the CEO's office. (How many of those do we need?) They were content to remain in their mid-level positions giving a little more than a fair day's work for a fair day's pay. Beyond that fair day's pay, the reward they most cherished was appreciation for helping to make work go smoothly for the people around them. Aren't these the workers companies need by the tens of millions?

I guess the reason I can't quite end this story is that for all my intellectual grasp of the downward trends for American workers, I just can't believe that these four generous/selfish, mellow/excitable, unique/ordinary, and highly employable individuals will simply remain the long-term unemployed. Even though they might.

Chapter Two

DOWN BY THE BANKS OF THE OHIO

Cash for Clunkers and XM Radio

In the second year of the Great Recession, the U.S. government granted a $4,200 rebate to anyone who bought a fuel-efficient new car and offered up an old one for sacrifice. My husband, Frank, and I brought in our twenty-year-old Lincoln Town Car and drove out with a brand-new Hyundai Elantra. It cost us $13,382, tax included.

Economically, it makes more sense to subsidize an embryonic industry than a mature industry, and public transit makes more environmental sense than private autos. Personally, I hoped for a weatherization/green jobs program to replace the leaky windows in the old industrial building where I live. But you take what you can get.

In our case Cash for Clunkers worked the way it was supposed to. It got a gas-guzzler off the road, and there's no other way we would have bought a new car. The program brought me a personal bonus besides. My new car introduced me to a father and son in Indiana who had been adjusting to the downturn for a generation before it hit the Pink Slip Club in New York. Here's how I met them.

Our new car came with a free trial subscription to XM Radio. Before it expired, several salesmen called offering low-rate deals to continue the service. My husband, Frank, said no to all of them. Then one day he said, "Okay, give me that." He was won over by a young man who said he knew how to make the discount subscription end automatically so we wouldn't find ourselves paying the full price when we forgot to cancel it in time.

"I got his number for you," Frank said when he got off the phone. "I figured anyone selling XM Radio from a call center had to be doing something better before the recession. He says he'd be happy to talk to you."

"I can't interview every underemployed American," I answered ungratefully. Still, I made a call.

"How long will we need?" Michael Kenny asked when I reached him at home on a weekend morning.

"I don't know," I said, dithering. "I don't usually interview on the phone."

"Why don't we go ahead and start discussing?" Michael said, amiably taking charge. "If we need to, we can continue on another day."

"Were you this good on the phone before you started doing it for a living?" I asked.

"Honestly, no, ma'am. Before my last two jobs I was very timid on the phone. I didn't even like to call and order pizza."

Before selling XM Radio, Michael, twenty-eight, had managed his fiancée's uncle's staffing agency. Most of its clients needed temporary loading crews for warehouses. Michael rounded up day laborers and sent them out at $7.50 an hour. But with the recession, business fell off for its clients (mostly low-end retailers), and the employment agency itself closed down.

The reason Michael might have to rush off the phone that morning was also recession related. He and his fiancée were looking at houses. The couple had been renting a house for the last five years, but the landlord stopped paying on the mortgage. "So we're faced with a notice to vacate."

"Oh no! First your job, then your home."

Michael assured me that it wasn't a tragedy. "We were already talking about having a child, and with house prices so low it's a good time to buy."

Michael's fiancée, Caitlin, was employed at a franchise print shop formerly owned by another uncle. It too had gone bankrupt. Fortunately, a rival print shop scooped up the machinery, the customers, and the fiancée. So Caitlin had an unbroken employment record. The couple decided it would look good if Michael was also employed when they went to get a mortgage.

"That's why I took the job at XM," he told me. He'd originally thought to stay for about a year. But now: "I've been there for a month and a half. I don't think I can take it for that long, honestly."

"How long did you work at the employment agency?" I asked.

"Five months, I guess. I took care of everything from payroll, getting the temps to the jobs, drug testing [of job applicants], all that kind of good stuff, plus answering the phones, billing. The boss came in for an hour or two to help with the billing, but really to use it as headquarters for the restaurant he owned. That closed too." Was I phoning a ghost town, I wondered, or were the uncles just jinxed?

I was surprised when Michael said he'd been unemployed for a full year between the temp agency and the call center.

"I'm only talking to you on the phone, but you sound so . . . employable."

"Well, I do need to tell you, ma'am, I have ten-year-old dreadlocks that hang down just to my waist. That does turn some employers off, especially here in the Midwest."

"Are you a Rastafarian?" I asked. I was also wondering if he was black. That might affect his job prospects.

"No, I'm not a Rastafarian. I respect women more than that. It's a spiritual thing with me. I'm actually a quarter Native American." (That didn't answer my hidden question. But he sounded like a white midwesterner.)

"It might be different if I was living in New York," Michael continued, "but the only jobs that were available to me here that year were fast foods, sandwich shops, stuff like that. And I just wasn't gonna go in reverse."

"Well, a call center, isn't that reverse? I mean, you were managing the employment agency."

"It is a bit of a reverse," he conceded. "But I am actually pulling in the same amount of money." At the call center Michael was paid $7.50 an hour plus $2.00 per sale. He estimates that he averages five sales a day, which brought it to about $72.00 a day.

"But it *is* a reverse in that I'm . . . I'm sacrificing some . . ." For the first time in our conversation, Michael Kenny groped for a word. "At the temp agency I really got a bit of . . . *satisfaction* [he found the word] because I was able to help someone find work.

"Like there was a single dad who was staying in a shelter with his two daughters. You could tell he was not someone who normally gets that close to the bottom. But his wife had passed away, and with the economy this time he fell all the way. So I gave him all the work I could . . . Mostly unloading trucks and moving boxes around. But that guy, he didn't care what it was. He just wanted to get his daughters out of the shelter.

"When I was able to help someone like that, it was a sense of satisfaction. I don't really get that out of XM Radio. I'll be honest with you, eight out of ten people we call, maybe nine out of ten people, it's kind of like we're hassling them. I'm supposed to push it and push it. They listen in for that. But I don't like hassling people. So it's kind of tough on me. I'll try to stay till we get a house."

"Why don't you buy the house you're renting?" I asked.

"It's not in the most beautiful neighborhood," he answered, "and we want to start a family. But it's not the ghetto, either." (Why was I too embarrassed to simply ask if he was black or white? It matters in America; it's an honest question.) "The identical house next door sold for $35,000," Michael reported. "They covered the hardwood floors, painted over the gorgeous woodwork, and resold it for $45,000. You could come to Evansville, buy this house, and rent it out."

"I don't even know where I'm calling. Evansville, is that near Chicago?"

"No, Evansville, Indiana. I'm literally right across the river from Kentucky."

"Oops, sorry."

"That's all right. I was born in the Chicago area. We moved here when I was three."

When I asked how his family got to Indiana, Michael launched into his father's life story. "My dad never went to college. *His* father left, and he had four brothers and sisters to help take care of. He worked two jobs and finished high school at night."

Mr. Kenny senior had taken a job with a national-brand food company "for the security." Michael represented his dad's thinking about security with emotions it was hard to interpret over the phone. The company had moved his father to Evansville, Michael said, and then downsized, leaving him stranded. So his dad got a job as a supervisor at the Indiana distribution center of a national retailer where he works to this day.

"Dad, he's been busting his hump working for these corporations for the last thirty-five years," Michael said. "He's actually the second-longest employee at this center, and yet they just put him on a night shift to try to force him out of the job. They even threatened to take his pension away from him at one point if he didn't quit. Someone actually said it to him: 'We'll fire you and take it away from you.'"

Michael went on with great feeling about the pressure his father worked under. "You know the way a corporation can scrutinize over you. When you supervise four hundred people, they can always find something that one of those people wasn't doing right that you should have caught. But he still didn't quit, and they still didn't fire him.

"My dad, he's resilient, he's right-on, but he hates what he does. It's paid his way—well, the job and credit cards. But it hasn't got him satisfaction. He finds that in church these days. I'm not going to live that way."

"Do you think your father would talk to me if I came to Evansville?" I surprised myself by saying.

Michael said he'd ask. A couple of weeks later he reported that his religious, Republican, and "right-on" dad was willing. (He really was a terrific salesman.) So we drove the new little car to Evansville, Indiana.

Michael and His Friends

At Michael's suggestion we checked into the Casino Aztar Hotel. The casino itself is a numbingly lit and Muzak-filled showboat, moored on the Ohio River. But the adjoining hotel offered double rooms for seniors at $39 a night. The senior discount must have been a real selling point because there were quite a few gamblers with walkers and portable oxygen tanks at the slot machines.

But the Aztar had just been bought by Tropicana Entertainment. A receptionist congratulated us on getting in under the wire. The senior rate was already scheduled to go up considerably, she told us.

"That's okay by me," I assured her, especially if it meant that her pay wouldn't go down too much. She said amen to that and explained that after the last cuts she'd moved her family across the river to Kentucky. But she wasn't going to find any place cheaper to live than that, she said.

His fiancée, Caitlin, was still working at the print shop, but Michael had quit the XM call center to spend time fixing up the house they'd just bought. It cost $95,000, and Caitlin had put all of the $20,000 that her grandmother had left her into a down payment so that they could get a low, fixed-rate, twenty-year loan. "Caitlin is very good with money," Michael said. She was determined never to refinance their house. Indeed the couple feared debt so strongly that "we don't possess a single credit card."

We were to meet at the new house as soon as Michael got back from driving a friend to a job interview. Though it was only an eight-minute ride from downtown, it was set in a cluster of old, rural-feeling houses circling a pond. Michael was relaxing on the porch when we arrived.

Michael Kenny turns out to be a blue-eyed, brown-haired midwesterner. The three-quarters of him that aren't American Indian are Irish and German. As for the dreadlocks, perhaps because he'd warned us or because they were so neatly tied back, the young man who stepped off the porch seemed not only presentable but winsome as he showed us the work he'd already done on the lawn.

"By the way, I found someone who'll hire me with my hair."

"Who?" I asked.

"Me. I'm hiring myself." Michael had designed and was planning to manufacture T-shirts for Deadheads to sell at Grateful Dead concerts. He'd already applied to incorporate the new T-shirt business.

Michael had been a hard-core Deadhead in his younger days, following the band from city to city on their tours. It was among fellow Deadheads that he noticed the fellowship among dreadlock wearers and started growing his. He showed me how the hair was allowed to tangle for months before being separated into the strong "roots" that remain forever untouched. Michael's roots hadn't been re-rolled for over nine years. "My energy is carried in my hair. Everything I've done in my last decade is with me. Here, pull," he said, showing me how strong his scalp had become.

One of the things that had impressed Michael about my husband was that Frank had actually photographed Jerry Garcia. "I never saw Jerry myself," Michael said with regret, "but Caitlin did."

"You know who else did?" I asked and explained that when I lived in San Francisco in the 1960s, friends had repeatedly tried to drag me over to a house in the Haight where this cool band rehearsed in public and anyone could go in and listen. When I finally went, I ran out screaming, "This is too noisy! I can't stand it!"

"That must have been before their acoustic period," Michael said tactfully. Rather than dismiss me as the most uncool person on the planet, he brought his guitar out on the porch and played a couple of Jerry Garcia's children's songs. He has a very pleasant voice, and he chose some nice safe songs for me. I liked them.

Michael took me inside to see a photograph of the Grateful Dead in front of their house at 710 Ashbury Street. "Yes," I remembered, "that looks like the place."

The guitar playing, the T-shirt art, the laid-back young man on the porch all brought back San Francisco in the 1960s. But Michael Kenny wasn't just a retro hippie. He was also an up-to-date hippie. The T-shirts he designed with the Dead's lightning bolt logo were strictly 1960s, of course. But the artwork that Michael was setting out, most by friends, included magnified photographs of microscopic glass cuttings and various up-to-date electronic crafts. It was a lot more skillful than the tie-dyes I remember from the 1960s.

The housewares Michael was unpacking were also contemporary hippie. His things were gathered and artistically embellished from today's discards, not from the already vintage or collectible. Bohemians of all eras have always preferred the unpolished and the unmatched. It allows them to scrounge aesthetically satisfying furnishings while limiting financial ties to "the system."

But even though one abjures wall-to-wall carpeting and suites of furniture, some hard currency is always needed. In the 1960s, even on a rural commune, there was always someone who put on high heels and stockings—it was usually a woman, as I remember—and went out to earn cash. In those days one could easily drop in and out of such employments, so we took turns. But Caitlin held one of the rare nine-to-five jobs in her circle. So while she worked a permanent, full-time job, the couple's less steadily employed friends made the new house their gathering place.

Shortly after I arrived, Bean, a tall, lanky youth, dropped a friend, Pete, off and exchanged a few words with Michael about the set Michael's group would play that evening at a local pub. He spoke through the kitchen screen door.

"You gotta go to work?" Michael asked.

"Yeah," Bean said with a sigh, and split.

"Boy, he looks sad," I said. "What kind of job?"

"He'll be tossing pizzas for the rest of the night," Michael answered. Then he said to Pete, "He picked up a double [shift] yesterday. He must really need the money."

Pete, an old high school friend of Michael's, had been back in town for two weeks. He was heavyset and also in his twenties, but he already had a former wife who had remarried and moved to Florida with her new husband and Pete's daughter. With not much going on in Evansville, Pete relocated to be near his child. But after nine months he hadn't found work in Florida, so he moved back. In his own words, "I'm kind of in between things."

Michael asked his friend about his job-search methods, ignored Pete's evasive reply, and delivered these pointers.

"The Internet is pretty much how you have to find a job these days. You can't go out and pound the pavement like we did ten years ago. Then, if you put in five, six applications a day and had decent references and were willing to work in restaurants with high turnover, you could find a job in three, four days. Now you can't put in applications in person anywhere, unless it's McDonald's."

Michael's description of the job search when he first got out of high school reminded me that even ten years before the Great Recession it had already been harder to pick up casual jobs than when I was young.

Michael described the futile feeling you got from Internet job hunting.

"For one thing, they never list the name of the company. A restaurant, they'll just say, kitchen job available; line cook; the pay per hour, the hours, and the skill set that they want—that's all. You send them your résumé; if they don't need you, you'll never hear back from them.

"Look, you can try the Internet thing," he said to Pete. "Or you can put in an application with one of the staffing agencies." (The friend Michael drove to a staffing agency that morning was a single mother who had been laid off from the plastics factory, one of the diminishing number of large manufacturers left in town. She was signing up at an agency for immediate shifts of warehouse work. "It's the same loading job I sent that father in the shelter to," Michael reminded me. "It's hard on your body: the quotas are always going up; but she needs the cash right away.")

"But the best place in town for anybody that needs money," Michael now instructed Pete, "while you're looking for the job, is go down to XM Radio, take the two-day training course, learn the computer system, and sit there in a comfy seat and talk on the phone all day.

"He likes talking," Michael said to me. I'd seen no sign of that.

"He likes computers." That might be true. "But he doesn't think he'd be good at it. But if you only do it for a couple, three weeks, that's four, five hundred dollars, and that gives you a little bit of money to hold on till you find other jobs.

"Plus, it gets you back into working again, gives you a schedule, makes you feel good. That's the thing about a daily job that I really miss. Working on my own ideas for years and sometimes procrastinating—definitely procrastinating—it's caused me to suffer when I could have been doing something that . . ." Michael couldn't quite finish his thought. "They're always hiring at XM," he concluded.

Pete said nothing.

I asked Michael if many of his friends were "in between things," like Pete and Bean. He told me proudly about his close friend, Bob. Through his mother, Bob got an apprenticeship with a sculptor who had a commission to build a metal fence—"an artistic fence"—for the city. When the apprenticeship ended, Bob returned to the usual dead-end jobs punctuated by long stints of unemployment. Then, because of the metal-fabricating skills he'd acquired, and through a lucky contact with the Masons, Bob got a job earning $18 an hour for a company that makes natural gas combustion chambers. "It required him to understand schematics, which he picked up like that. Bob is brilliant," Michael said.

"He's had that job for *two* years. And to see him over that time go from working behind a hotel desk, running the place all night, and only making $8.50 an hour to working his way into a machine shop where they do very high-tech and precise work.

"He owns his own car that's paid off. He lives in his own apartment that he doesn't have to worry about paying for every month because his job covers his bills. He's got *in*surance, and everything is completely turned around for him. It's a rare story. I'm very happy for him. Very proud."

To hear Michael talk, you'd think his friends were drug addicts or ex-cons. What his brilliant friend Bob has is a steady job at a living wage. A full-time job at $18.50 an hour is $36,000.00 a year—enough to support a single guy or even a family if the wife brings something in. Yet for Michael it was the epitome of success. Pete thought so too.

Maybe I have to reconsider the word "hippie" for Michael and his friends. In the 1960s my hippie friends made a conscious life-style choice. They dropped out of financially and socially rewarding careers to do something more "meaningful." That included meaningfully chilling out.

Michael and his friends seem to have arrived at the hippie ethic from another direction. They don't have the option of well-paying, steady jobs. But they do have the option of not feeling bad about that.

Over the course of a long afternoon Michael and I, both great digressers, discussed many things and people. But two men came up repeatedly.

Ever since our phone conversation, I'd been thinking about the widower who had been living in the shelter with his children.

"I don't remember his name," Michael said, "but I remember he couldn't be here till seven—which was a half an hour late—because he had to get his kids to the bus stop. He couldn't leave them at the shelter unattended, you know. So I worked it out for him to where he could get his girls to the bus stop in the morning and be off in time to pick them up there as well.

"I felt very good about that. That was my satisfaction. But now I think, 'How was he going to pay rent and food and get the heat and electric turned on on $7.50 an hour?'

"Something that I feel sick about—and it's not to look down on anybody who runs a staffing agency, it's just the business—but a staffing agency gets paid probably $12.00 to $14.00 an hour, and they only hand over $7.50 an hour. That's almost half the amount we take from these people that go work these jobs that hardly any of us would want to do. But the companies would rather pay us $5.00 an hour, per person, just so they don't have to deal with them." Michael sometimes sent out an entire temp crew with its own foreman. No one from the client company had to speak directly to the day laborer.

"At first I felt good about giving people like that jobs. Then I started to feel bad. I see them drag in at the end of the shift for their checks, and all I see is the number 56. Fifty-six dollars is the check for a full shift. How is someone going to pay rent and utilities on $56.00? So how was I helping him get his children out of the shelter?"

"Michael," I asked, "at $7.50 an hour for an eight-hour shift, shouldn't that be *$60.00*?"

"They get a half-hour lunch break."

"Oh my God, they deduct for lunch!" I thought about the bleakness of that unpaid break in a warehouse canteen. The chips in the snack machines were probably stale.

It was I who asked about that single father, but it was Michael who continually brought his own father into our conversation and always with intense emotion.

"My dad started as a supervisor; now he's a manager. But they could pay a guy my age, just out of college, half the money they're paying him. So they've been trying to force him out for the last five years."

Michael admires his father: "He's a tough man. He knows how to take it on the chin."

But, though he doesn't quite say it, I think he also feels his father was a sucker. "My dad says I don't know how to stick with anything. All I know is I don't want to end up putting in twenty, twenty-five years in a place and have them trying to toss me out on my butt."

I hadn't yet met Mr. Kenny, but out of generational loyalty I wanted the son to understand that people like his father weren't just saps who played by the rules in a game everyone else knew was fixed.

"There used to be an understanding between employer and employee," I began my history lesson. "At the time your father chose a corporate career, no one would have fired a lifetime employee to chisel him out of his pension or to replace him with a kid half his age. When businesses were expanding, they took in the young and kept the old.

"Sometimes a company man might say to himself, 'Look what I've done: I've wasted my life for security.' But at least he got the security. That contract was changed behind your father's back."

"Right! I've been telling that to my dad for years, and it seems like he *just* recently realized it. He recently told me he'd be happier working on my brother-in-law's farm for $10 an hour."

Michael was determined to play by different rules yet win his father's approval nonetheless. "He feels I could do better. He knows I'm capable of more. But at the same time he *hates* his job and where he's at. Obviously, his job made him some money," Michael conceded. "He took good care of me and my sister: he kept up a middle-class life. But . . .

"I think he's changing his position on what I should do. I think he wants me to take my time and find out what's right for me. He just wants me to cut my hair and make money in the meantime."

I smiled at that and Michael did too.

Before we parted, Michael took us for a ride around town. The working-class sitcom *Roseanne*, which starred Roseanne Barr, had been created by a fellow who went to Michael's school. The street signs and working-class house exteriors seen briefly in each episode are Evansville tourist attractions. Next we stopped at Michael and Caitlin's foreclosed former home. It was on a block of wooden houses a bit smaller, older, and shabbier than Roseanne's. The house was still vacant, and Michael was visibly distressed to see it so uncared for. Then we drove into a black neighborhood past the employment agency that Michael had managed. The ramshackle dwelling that had housed the agency was vacant and derelict.

When we stopped for gas, I handed Michael my credit card, but he didn't know what to do with it. I was amazed that an American male didn't know how to swipe a credit card at a gas pump. But Michael and Caitlin don't possess a single credit card, as he reminded me. "We always cut them up."

"Ask my dad about credit cards when you talk to him," Michael advised me. I made a note. "And enjoy the new couch," he added mysteriously.

The Pigeon Township Trustee

We had a free day before our appointment with Mr. Kenny senior. I decided to play detective and track down that single father whom Michael tried to help. All I knew was that his wife had died and that during the time Michael was sending him out on loading crews, he and his two daughters lived in a homeless shelter.

The YWCA, my first stop, was a shelter for victims of domestic violence. They would never have permitted a man in the residential area, even with two girl children, the receptionist told us. But she gave me a list of local food pantries and shelters.

We stopped at a men's shelter where the people sitting around looked like your classic winos. The director couldn't remember a man coming in with children, and, besides, "it wouldn't be a suitable place."

According to the director, his resident population hadn't changed with the recession. But in addition to beds for men, they offered meals and the free use of their laundry rooms to anyone who came in during the day. "Many, many more women with children are using these things since the recession," he said.

In times of economic crisis or natural disaster the job of scavenging almost always falls on women. In looking for that single father, I was concentrating on the statistical exception.

After a couple of stops it became apparent that the only Evansville shelter likely to take in a man with two children was the Dorothea MacGregor Family Shelter, run by the Pigeon Township Trustee.

The township trustee is an elected official who oversees what is still called "poor relief." According to a brochure aimed at potential applicants, one must, in order to get aid, "be in need of essentials of life" and "be willing to help yourself as much as possible." If those conditions were met, the Trustee's Office could provide vouchers ("*never cash*," the brochure emphasized) for goods and services like cleaning supplies and dental work.

The trustee's drab prefab office was across the street from a cheery yellow house that had been divided into apartments. I asked the receptionist an open-ended question about current relief needs. One recent problem, she said, was that the utilities company, Vectren, had reorganized their records so that they can now spot people who owed back bills in other counties. "So now we're seeing people who can't get rehoused because they can't get utilities turned on in their own name unless they work out a way to pay off a back bill that could be $1,200 to $1,400 or more."

Since speaking to Michael, I had become adept at dividing and multiplying by 56—the standard daily wage he paid for a full warehouse shift. I calculated that it would take 21.4 such shifts to pay off a utility bill of $1,200, assuming you didn't spend any money on food. And surely the utility company would require a new deposit before it'd turn a deadbeat on again.

"Where I live, the landlord pays the heating bills," I said. "I'm just beginning to understand that people paying $700 a month rent in Evansville may have to pay $200 a month for utilities."

"It might be closer to $300 to heat the run-down, leaky places they're likely to find," the woman said.

She took me in to see the Pigeon Township Trustee, Mary Hart, who had the first really southern accent I'd heard in southern Indiana. Ms. Hart had mastered the art of being both direct and gracious at the same time. And she didn't mind if I turned on my tape recorder.

Ms. Hart confirmed that an increasing number of people ready to move into new housing were coming to the township for shelter because they couldn't get their electricity turned back on. One of her jobs was to negotiate installment plans with the utility company and help applicants work out a budget that would allow them to keep up their payments.

"Do you sometimes have to tell people you can't have both utilities and a car?"

"Worse than that," Mary answered, "sometimes it's either pay the rent or pay for the medicine for a sick child. If they buy the medicine, then they fall behind on the rent. And because they're living paycheck to paycheck, once they fall behind, they can never catch up. And that's where the township trustee comes into play because we'll tell them, 'You keep paying the rent, and we'll get the child's medicine.'"

As to the car-or-utilities choice: "We will say, your family can't afford *two* cars. But they will almost always need one car to get to work."

At the time I was in Evansville, the media was still talking about recent mass layoffs at Whirlpool. I asked Ms. Hart how the trustees plan for something like that. The yellow house could shelter only a few families at a time.

"We knew a year in advance that there were going to be eleven hundred people losing their jobs at Whirlpool when they moved work from here to Mexico. So we planned for people coming to us. Actually, we haven't seen the Whirlpool homeless yet, because they gave them a pretty good severance package plus they offered some retraining. We see from the feeder plants first. Not Whirlpool, but those smaller places that supply the rubber gaskets or other parts to Whirlpool. They also laid people off."

"Do you really see it that directly?" I asked. "Here's the layoff, here come the people."

"Yes," Mary said. "We ask the place of last employment. It's on our application. So we know whether it was a feeder into Whirlpool or Whirlpool workers themselves. A couple of years ago, when the casino business got bad, Casino Aztar laid off about sixty people. We felt the effect immediately; they came through our door right away.

"It's the smaller companies," Ms. Hart said. "One of the staffing companies, Custom Staffing, closed down [that was not Michael's firm] and merged with another company a year ago. We felt the effect right away. People came in who, they may have found another job for $7.50 an hour, but they may now only be working thirty hours a week. So now with their bring-home pay, they can either pay the rent or pay the utilities, but they can't do both. Or they get sick. They need a tooth extraction in order to continue going to work. We arrange the tooth extractions."

"Ms. Hart," I said, "everywhere I go here people tell me about $15.00-an-hour jobs that left Evansville, but I only see $7.50 jobs coming in. How can the trusteeship help a man if, even after he gets full-time work, he won't earn enough to pay for the basic necessities?"

"At that point, we may also try to assist him into getting into public housing. If we see his problem is going to become long-term, we try to get them into a housing situation where you pay 30 percent [of their family income for rent]. Our clients take top priority in the public housing situation."

But all that does is subsidize below living wages, I thought to myself. And as to moving the deserving poor into public housing, who are you going to move out?

"We have a great need for affordable housing in this community," Ms. Hart said, perhaps following my thoughts. "On any given night we will have 456 to 463 on the street, and about a third of them are children. Parks, bus stations, or vehicles.

"We'll always have a homeless population because of drug abuse, mental instability, but the others . . ." I leveled with Mary. It was only those "others" I was interested in. I hope that the trustees' intervention makes life a little less painful for the children of drug addicts and manic-depressives. But cruel as it sounds, really damaged people are not my focus.

I told Ms. Hart about the father with two girls who'd found himself in a shelter after his wife died. I also told her about the young man at the temp agency who wanted to believe he was helping that family get back to a normal life by sending the man out on $7.50-an-hour jobs.

"I know you can't give me individual names," I said, "but I was wondering how he made out. How does a man like that get his family out of a shelter and back into a regular home?"

Ms. Hart said that the trustees had housed more than one single man with children since the recession started. In fact, when I got home, they put me in touch with one whose wife had died. But he turned out to be the wrong man.

Meanwhile, it was time to meet Michael's dad.

Religious, Republican, and Right-On

Michael's dad, Chuck, is a stiff, sturdy, short man who wore a crisp checked shirt and crease-free jeans. He welcomed us into a three-bedroom, two-bath tract home where everything had its place and hadn't been put there just for our visit.

The only things lying around were a book on the television

and an amplifier left out for Michael. Chuck had recently gotten a larger one to use with his guitar at church.

I sensed that this man had no idea what I wanted with him. It was trusting of him to accommodate his son this way. So I began by assuring him that I don't use real names and I try to be vague about places of employment. "I'll probably just say that you work in the warehouse of a . . ."

"Distribution center," he corrected me for the sake of accuracy.

". . . in the distribution center of a big-box store that I'll call Big Box."

"It's where I got these socks," my husband said.

"My jeans, my socks, my underwear, come from there too," said Mr. Kenny. "But it's an Eddie Bauer shirt. I like nice things, and I don't like to iron."

Once Frank and Michael had left, Mr. Kenny fell to talking about his son. "Michael is so smart; he could do so many things." The father and son were equally wrapped up in each other. "I tell him if he just . . ."

The phone rang. It was his grandchildren, and Mr. Kenny was soon smiling so broadly that I thought his cheeks must ache.

"Hi, sweetheart. You miss Pawh-Pawh? . . . Okay, put 'em on . . ."

While Chuck spoke about report cards with one of his older grandchildren—"That's an improvement"—I looked around the living room. It was dominated by two large portraits over the fireplace—one of Michael and one of his stepsister, the mother of those grandchildren on the phone. In his early teens Michael had had bird-downy hair that one could hardly resist fluffing.

By the time Mr. Kenny hung up, I was examining the book he

was reading, Karl Rove's *Courage and Consequence: My Life as a Conservative in the Fight.*

"Michael and I don't share political opinions," he said, "but we share how we love people."

I asked Mr. Kenny about his work history.

"I've never been unemployed since I was twelve years old," he answered. I knew from his son that Chuck had taken on a lot of financial responsibility when his father left the family. Mr. Kenny gave me a more neutral chronology that included military service ("during the Vietnam War but not in Vietnam"), full-time jobs during an early marriage ("Ellen and I have been married thirty-three years," he was anxious to tell me about his second wife), a corporate downsizing, a brief return to work for a family business ("owned by a Jewish family that I'd left on good terms"), and finally: "Twenty-four years ago yesterday, I went to work for Big Box, and I've been there ever since. I had opportunities to go other places. It's sort of ironic, because I'm working a strange shift right now. But the reason I never left Big Box is because I was always able to be on days there, which left me the evenings and the weekends for my family and one of my hobbies, which is refereeing soccer.

"With the shift I'm on right now," Mr. Kenny said, "I can't referee soccer on the weekends if I want to spend any time with my family."

"Michael says that you worked all these years for this company and now they'd like a cheaper payroll—that's Michael's interpretation—so they put you on a shift they hoped you'd quit."

"Trying to bring younger people in, forcing the older people out; it's a constant battle. Fortunately, I've been able to survive. I don't put stock in my *own* abilities to maintain that employment. I truly believe it's through the grace of God and the strength and perseverance He gives me to say the right things to the right people.

"I had to tell a vice president once that I'm trying to do my work as if I was doing it for my Creator. If that makes you happy, I'm happy. If it doesn't, I'll just go over somewhere else."

"And yet you've stayed?"

"I've stayed. I've worked under eight facility vice presidents. They average about three years apiece."

Chuck's son-in-law and stepdaughter raise two thousand acres of feed corn and soybeans on a farm that's been in the son-in-law's family since the nineteenth century. The previous fall the couple had to be in Russia by Thanksgiving to meet the child they were adopting. (The very granddaughter, now two years old, whom Pawh-Pawh just spoke to on the phone.) "But we had a real wet fall, so they got a late start on harvest, and it was all hands on deck."

"And you helped in the fields?"

"I learned to drive tractors, semis, grain trucks, taking them down to the river to . . ."

"That smile again," I said. "It's almost like your grandchild's smile."

"Yeah, and we got to be out there with the grandchildren. Worked long hours; got this camaraderie—my son-in-law, his brother, my best friend, Len, who was a vice president at a paint company who got downsized. Our church people would come out and drive trucks and . . . I get emotional," Mr. Kenny apologized, "but friends, church farmers, all came to help. We finished four days before they had to go to Russia."

"Michael says you're thinking of retiring and working on the farm?"

"Yes, being a hired hand."

"That's hard work."

"It's hard work, but at least you get to work with people you truly, truly care about. I have good relations with my longtime co-workers at Big Box," he hastened to say, "but they're not my family."

In gross outline, retailers like Big Box import huge shipments of goods from Asia and disperse them in smaller lots from depots around the United States. In the area that Chuck manages, seven supervisors oversee about two hundred hourly associates who sort, mark, and ticket merchandise, then send it back out in the assortments of colors and sizes appropriate for each of their stores in the region.

It occurred to me that most of this could be done on the Asian end without an intermediate stop at a distribution center in Indiana. Maybe it will be eventually. In the meantime, the company had just done an old-fashioned time-and-motion study—how many seconds to open the first flap of this or that carton, how many seconds to unclip a tag, fold a sleeve, and so on. This resulted in new quotas that had already been implemented in other Big Box distribution centers. "They're already getting it done with less people at lower cost," Chuck said. "So now the pressure is on us to get up there."

Along with new quotas the company had instituted a change from a five-day week to a ten-hour-a-day, four-day week.

"Four tens means management's got to be there 2:30 in the afternoon," Chuck explained. "And we don't get off till about 3:30 in the morning."

"That's over twelve hours!" I said.

"Right. Management does thirteen hours for the ten-hour shift. If the shift goes overtime, we're there till five o'clock in the morning. And if they work on Friday, then it's not a four-day week; it's a five-day week. And you've already worked fifty-two hours. So it's now sixty hours. So you've given them another half week's work." Managers don't receive overtime pay.

Americans work longer hours than people in any other industrial country. We average 20 percent more, for instance, than French or German workers. That amounts to an extra day a week. Not only have Americans been working longer hours since the mid-1970s, but American families have been sending more members out to work. Michael's mother worked full-time as long as he could remember. Chuck says that in the families he knows at church, both spouses work "except if there's a problem like unemployment or illness."

If families are working so many more hours than in the past, why do they borrow so much? I didn't want to sound as if I were accusing the Kennys of extravagance or poor management. Nor did I want to put my own theories into his mouth. So I broached the subject of debt in as open-ended a manner as I could.

"I notice your son doesn't have a credit card. He almost won't touch one."

"I think Michael has learned from our mistakes," Mr. Kenny volunteered. "We, like all young families, used credit cards and got into debt."

"What kind of debt?" I asked. "What were you buying?"

"Just normal expenses. We were saying, 'Why should the two of us be working as hard as we are and not be able to afford a decent car or computers. Maybe we were keeping up with the Joneses. So you'd put it on your card. Then something would come up; you couldn't make the full payment, so you'd carry it over.

"There was a point in time when we had a lot of medical problems with our daughter and we had college debt with her: we were living paycheck to paycheck; it was getting to where I was having to wire money for a car payment so it wouldn't be late.

"At the time we weren't tithing," Mr. Kenny explained. "We were giving like 6 percent. And I remember one Sunday morning we were going to a church, and we were sort of having a heated discussion on the way. The kids weren't with us. I don't know what they were doing then, maybe just sleeping.

"My wife said, 'I think we should be tithing.' I said, 'We can hardly make our payments now, and you want to increase our giving?' She said, 'Yes.'

"Well, that Sunday when we wrote the check, she said, 'What will it be for?' I figured it out and wrote the check. And we have never been in need of money since then."

There was a long pause.

"I'm not saying money hasn't been tight. But we have not been living paycheck to paycheck since we decided to give God back a tenth of what he has given us."

"Do you remember what year that was?" I asked.

"It must have been about fifteen years ago because I had heart trouble right after that. They gave me angioplasty."

"How long since you've been out of debt?" I asked.

"Sometime in the last five years. Well, we still owe on our house, of course, and one vehicle and the new furniture you're sitting on." He gestured to the couch. "But that was interest-free," he said, hastening to set the record straight.

"It's very comfortable," I said. It must be the new couch Michael instructed me to "enjoy." "*Very* comfortable."

"We had the old one for twenty years," Mr. Kenny said, defending his purchase. "I could pay this off right now, but I'd have to go into my retirement savings. So I thought I'd just wait to give them the money since I can do it at no cost."

I could imagine how Michael derided the new couch bought on credit even though at no interest.

"One thing my faith has taught me," Mr. Kenny declared, "you cannot be a slave to two masters. Only one. With debt you're at the mercy of your employer. If they say 'You will do this,' you can't say 'No I won't: I'll just leave,' because you have bills to pay. And if you have bills, you're subject to the terms that job puts on you. Employers know that.

"But Michael has no debt. Who's he responsible to? He can pack up and go. If the Lord tells him to go to Nineveh like he told Jonah, he can go. When you're in debt, you can't do that."

What a thought! One's own son might be called to preach to Nineveh. Michael's unshorn locks may even be a sign of his readiness, for they make it difficult for him to be tied to an encumbering steady job. But what did this say about Chuck himself? Does he believe that the debt he'd incurred by dutifully taking care of so many people over his lifetime disqualified him from responding to God's call? It must be terrible for him to feel that way.

I asked Mr. Kenny if the long unreimbursed hours were because of the recession. "Does the company thank you for helping them through their downturn?"

"Big Box is doing extremely well financially," he asserted. "And they also own Medium Box [a more upscale chain]. We're just short-staffed."

Big Box and its parent company were indeed profitable. During 2010, the year I spoke to Chuck, they returned considerable money to shareholders through stock buybacks. The remaining shareholders enjoyed an increased rate of return on their capital while employing several thousand fewer workers. It may be a smaller company, but productivity—the value of output per paid hour—was up, and investors took a greater share of that in profit.

America's successful firms have traditionally increased labor productivity by giving their employees the most advanced equipment in the world to work with. Some automation may have been going on at Big Box. But at the distribution center, Chuck Kenny increased the company's productivity by the low-tech means of donating free days of work and by enduring the tension that comes from feeling understaffed.

I recently heard about a Walmart-owned warehouse in Elwood, Illinois, that's pioneered the practice of paying the loading crews on piecework. If they have to wait for a container, they can take home less than the minimum $7.50 an hour. Someone showed me the pay stub of a man who worked 12.5 hours for $57.81. This primitive form of increasing labor productivity actually militates against efficient scheduling and investment in new machinery. It's a third-world way of squeezing out profits.

Chuck Kenny is not a complainer. He was unhappy about the way he was being treated at Big Box. He's also regretful about his own career choices, and at his age these regrets are naturally on his mind. But he only talked to me about them because I asked. I didn't have to ask, however, to hear about God, the farm, or his grandchildren.

"I never realized being a grandparent was going to be like this," he said, welling up. "My grandchildren think I'm *it*. 'Pawh-Pawh.' The twins said that even before they said 'Mimi.' I've always been the one that was down on the floor with them. I'm the one that takes the boys out on the farm, into the woods, down to the creek. Adventures. And Isabella wants to do whatever the boys do."

The Kennys' church has a congregation of about a hundred. They'd been meeting in a school gymnasium till the housing bust gave them the chance to get property cheaply. Their new building was being renovated. But the same price decline that benefited the church put the kibosh on the Kennys' personal plans.

"We were going to build a house on the farm. They gave us three acres, we'd already settled on the plans, and we were just at the point to order materials. But it was 2007, and I just felt uneasy about the economy. We were talking about a long-term financial commitment, but the uncertainty about our jobs, our pensions . . ."

"Couldn't you sell this house to pay for building a house on the farm?" I suggested.

That's exactly what they'd intended, but Chuck Kenny said, "Right now our house is probably worth 40 percent less than it was ten years ago. A lot of people will buy a home and sell it at the right time and make a ton of money. Ellen and I have lived in two other houses before this, but we've never been able to do that. Well . . . that's the way it goes.

"We like this house," he said to console himself. "We've mortgaged it a couple of times with the kids in school. But by now, I don't mind telling you, it's only $895 a month. It would be nice to be near the grandchildren. Nice, but who wants a large new mortgage at the age of sixty? I think we made the right decision not to take on new debt."

For a lot of our remaining time we talked about Michael—how to get the bright young man well settled. Chuck knew his son's strengths and weaknesses, and he agonized over the right amount of help a parent should give—the right balance of carrot and stick.

He'd put $5,000 down on Michael's present car in order to get the monthly payments down to something Michael could afford. "You need a car to work." At Big Box, Chuck had seen people dismissed as too unsteady because they drove unreliable cars or depended on rides from family members.

"You want to help your children when they're helping themselves. But when they're not, you have to start pulling back. Maybe if I had started pulling back a little earlier, he would be a little further ahead right now."

"We just can't know," I said.

"No, you don't know. I tell him, 'Cut your hair and get a job.' He drives me crazy and I push back. But he's gonna live his life his way."

"What about Michael's friends?" I asked. The Kennys had taken in a couple of their children's schoolmates during rough patches in life like parents divorcing. "I heard Michael tell a friend back from Florida that you can't just pound the pavement for a job these days. So where should they go?"

"Take the fast-food industry," Mr. Kenny replied. "You go to work in McDonald's; you apply yourself; you can get into their management program. Big Box hired several fast-food managers as supervisors because they have experience where it's fast paced, quick, and very regimented. Those skills are transferable. But first you have to be willing to put on the hairnet and do the work."

Here's a man who knows the Evansville labor market. His idea of a career path for a kid like his son starts by putting on the hairnet at McDonald's with the hope of transferring that discipline to a warehouse management job like the one he started with.

With perseverance and luck or God's help to say the right things, that young man might move up to the job Mr. Kenny himself holds now—a job where he keeps working longer hours for the same salary. Where, in other words, his hourly wage has been going down. But isn't each generation of Americans supposed to move up in the world?

His employers hadn't repaid Chuck Kenny's loyalty with their own, yet he didn't have much respect, or at least much hope, for any friend of Michael's who couldn't bite the bullet and pursue the only employment opportunities that were really out there: fast food and Big Box.

That doesn't mean you don't try to find something better for your own child. After all, "Michael is so bright." And even if he weren't, each parent's job is to help his own particular children to beat the odds.

We went round in circles about what Michael might do till Mr. Kenny took a phone call and returned restless or distressed. It was time for work, and he was headed for a long shift at a place where his staff was under pressure to meet new quotas and he was under personal pressure to leave. Who knew what additional pressure he learned about in that phone call? Chuck Kenny set off on a brilliant fall afternoon and wouldn't get home until almost five in the morning.

"What Am I Looking at Here in Evansville?"

Our $39 room at the Aztar overlooked the Ohio River. Each morning we'd seen at least one dog walker, but never more than two, on the new downtown promenade. We'd also seen three cyclists using the bike path. With our business just about wrapped up, we decided to check out the redevelopment area.

We strolled the three blocks of Evansville's newly gentrified Main Street, wondering which empty gourmet coffee shop to patronize. We saw a young woman go into one of them, and Frank caught a glimpse of a union logo on her T-shirt. So we followed and asked her where we could learn a little about the town's labor history. She directed us to Charles A. Whobrey, president and business manager of Teamster Local 215. A walk farther down Main through the old, somewhat more peopled downtown brought us to the Teamsters headquarters building on Walnut Street.

"What am I looking at here in Evansville?" I asked the lean fifty-year-old as he led us into his cubbyhole of an office. "How could a town have gotten this depressed since Lehman Brothers collapsed?"

"You're not looking at the effects of just *this* recession," he asserted. "So many people here survive paycheck to paycheck, obviously living beyond their means, that when something like this hits . . . well, let me go back.

"I started working for the union in 1981." Whobrey's Kentucky hills accent broadened as he got into his story. "I started in March, and not a month later President Reagan fired the air traffic controllers. Permanently fired the strikers. That doesn't happen much in American history. Killing PATCO [the air traffic controllers' union] sent the signal to business—as it was supposed to—that it was okay to get rid of the unions. 'Uh-oh,' I said, 'I have the knack for gettin' involved right when the wheel's going into the mud.'"

And with unions went wages.

"We used to have plenty of people around Evansville making $15, $21, $25 an hour. Those are people that can survive through a recession.

"Okay, so you take a 15 percent temporary pay cut—like we just gave. Our members could hold out till times got better. But now the middle-class worker starts out in debt. They have nothing to fall back on. So you're not looking at just this recession, you're looking at the cumulative effect of at least thirty years that started when I joined the labor movement and Reagan broke PATCO."

At least Whobrey had recognized a historic turning point when he saw it. I'd covered the PATCO strike as a reporter, and I hadn't.

The article I wrote explaining the strikers' grievance—not money, but hours and stress, the same complaints as today's air traffic controllers—was killed by the paper that assigned it. In its place the *Village Voice* ran a front-page essay about PATCO in which a hip black journalist reviled those white men (which they almost all were) making $50,000 a year (which they almost all weren't) who were in a position to tie up the country's airports (which it turned out they couldn't).

This was the first time I'd had an article killed. It should have alerted me to how profoundly the entire nation was being lined up against unions. I assumed, instead, that the article wasn't quite up to my standards. And it wasn't. For unlike Whobrey, I hadn't spotted this as the very moment that the wheel went into the mud.

Between then and now, Whobrey's southern Indiana Teamsters local declined from five thousand to three thousand members. "And we're doing better than most," he said.

"One of our guys out of work got a job driving hazardous material, explosives, I think. Anyway, he's got a hazmat license, but he got $12 an hour and no benefits. Oh yes, they gave him an IRA, and they'll match anything he puts in up to 6 percent of his pay. What they don't say is they won't pay you enough to put anything in. So they don't have anything to match, and you don't have any pension."

In a Monday morning quarterback kind of way, Whobrey and I wondered what would have happened if stronger airport unions had gone out to defend the amateurish air traffic controllers. Would solidarity at the start have staved off thirty years of decline? That kind of speculation is both useless and endless.

It was after five when Chuck Whobrey let us out of the Teamsters building onto an empty downtown street.

"So what you're looking at in Evansville," he said, ending where he started, "it's not the result of just this recession. It's the effect of thirty years since the wheel went into the mud for American workers."

Father and Son Philosophies

Whobrey is right. What I saw on the streets of Evansville was not the result of one deep recession but the cumulative effects of a much longer downturn for American workers. But what started that downturn?

From the end of World War II until the 1970s the United States enjoyed a quarter of a century of shared prosperity. Corporate profits rose steadily, and so did the wages of a working class that called itself "the middle class."

Then the sharing petered out. Between 1976 and 2007, 58 percent of every new dollar of income generated went to the top 1 percent of households. Economists suggest many triggers for the Great Reversal. They fall roughly into two categories.

The majority of economists point to specific pressures on profitability like the oil price shock of 1973 and competition from newly rebuilt Germany and Japan. The argument goes that as the sole industrial power to survive World War II intact, the United States had grown complacent about modernizing while Germany and Japan built almost everything brand-new. As soon as profit rates dipped at home, our alert financiers helped expand competition further by moving money abroad, including some to the countries that would soon become known as the Asian Tigers.

Whichever specific pressures to profitability they emphasize, these economists agree that U.S. profits fell (or started to stop growing) in the early to mid-1970s. By the 1980s employers became serious about cutting labor costs.

A smaller group of economists explain the Great Reversal primarily as a political phenomenon. By the mid-1970s, they say, the lessons of the Great Depression had been almost forgotten—except by a few diehards who'd been waiting for the chance to undo the New Deal. By the 1980s this group, buoyed by neoliberal sentiment, was powerful enough to elect politicians like Ronald Reagan and Margaret Thatcher who weakened unions at home and made it easier to move work abroad. These and subsequent administrations redistributed wealth upward through tax "reform" and, in the 1990s and first decade of the twenty-first century, through privatization, deregulation, and the end of capital controls. In other words, a political sea change freed capitalists to act as they always would if you remove the restrictions.

To oversimplify the differences only a little: one side says they did it because they *had to*; the other side says they did it because they *could*.

My own view is that real challenges to profitability surfaced in the 1970s. But the balance of political power determined that these many-faceted economic problems would be tackled primarily by cutting labor costs. There would be no more sharing of the ups and downs.

However complex and debatable the causes, it's clear that starting around the mid-1970s, the wealth gap widened while hourly wages stagnated or declined.

If couples wanted to maintain homes like the ones they were raised in, they borrowed and/or took second jobs. This left many families with both unmanageable children and unmanageable debts.

Chuck Kenny accuses himself of trying to keep up with the Joneses. But I don't think Chuck was trying to keep up with the Joneses next door. He was trying to keep up with the Joneses of a generation earlier. Since his father had deserted the family, Chuck's image of middle-class life may have come from television. But for most Americans—white Americans, at least—those imaginary TV families of the 1950s were statistically real.

A blue-collar worker like William Bendix in *The Life of Riley* could own a modest home, buy a television (far more costly for its time than a computer today), take his family on camping vacations, and send a boy to college in preparation for a job that would pay better than his father's and actually existed.

A professional or middle manager like Chuck Kenny could own a ranch home, take more expensive vacations, trade a car in every few years, then send the boy *and* the girl to college. For unless you were incompetent or unlucky, your earnings gradually increased over the course of your working life.

That had already begun to change when Chuck Kenny entered the workforce. But it's hard for any of us to appreciate how a gradual decline affects us day to day.

Mr. Kenny knows that things haven't turned out as they were supposed to. Even on two incomes, he and his wife couldn't put two children through college and then glide into a debt-free retirement. But after 150 years of objectively moving up, we Americans perceive of our country as a land of opportunity. Each couple is bound to think that its personal stagnation rests on personal limitations or mistakes.

Other people bought and sold houses at the right time, Chuck reminded me. And he had opted for the security of a large corporation when he might have stayed with that small business where they wouldn't get rid of an older worker just to lower the payroll.

Chuck worries that Big Box is after him because he can't cut the mustard anymore. He'd mentioned to me, almost in a whisper, that he doesn't take to the computer the way the young people do. He must also have the unavoidable suspicion—this must be difficult to express, even to one's wife—that he hasn't achieved all he might have because he's just not a top-notch individual.

The Kennys may indeed have failed to grasp opportunities that would leapfrog them over others. But their basic economic mistake was to assume that salaries, house prices, and savings would gradually increase over the years. In other words, the Kennys fell behind because they didn't fully grasp that they *weren't going to get ahead*.

But adjusting to downward mobility would have required a midlife course correction that's inimical to Americans of their generation. As I've said, down is an un-American direction.

Their son, Michael, on the other hand, was born on the down escalator. Since childhood he'd watched his parents running to stay in place. His mother had recently managed to keep her job when her company merged with another organization and downsized. She now supervises more people and works longer hours for the same money, Michael told me. Both at home and at the staffing agency Michael saw employers raising quotas and beating down wages. It has been going on as long as he can remember.

In this long and one-sided class war, Michael Kenny has declared himself a noncombatant. You won't catch him struggling to maintain a higher standard of living on a declining wage. And what sort of fool borrows to get things he can't afford now, when his future income is bound to be the same or lower? Michael won't flail like his father to maintain a middle-class lifestyle; he'll go with the flow.

However frustrating it is to his parents, his neo-hippie lifestyle makes sense. "Do your own thing" can be a comforting mantra when you can't afford matching furniture anyway.

A Different Generation Gap

There's an obvious generation gap between Chuck and Michael Kenny. They're father and son, after all. But there's another kind of generation gap between these Indiana folks and the Pink Slip Clubbers of New York.

When factories started closing or moving abroad in the 1970s and 1980s, we were told not to worry. Yes, some blue-collar workers might have to be pensioned off. But the rest of us would become "information workers" in the "postindustrial society." The important thing was to acquire the skills of the future.

The four Pink Slippers prepared themselves appropriately for careers in symbol manipulation. Yet Feldman, the graphics man, worked for many years as an hourly temp. Like teaching French literature by the semester or writing computer code by the line, not only do you take home less as a contingent worker, but you're outside the company and somehow outside the society.

The other three Pink Slippers did brain work that requires a great deal of initiative and involves too much interaction with people here to be easily outsourced to some other English-speaking country. Still they had seen their real pay stagnate and some benefits, like pensions, fade away.

Something bad has been creeping up the occupational ladder. First it hit blue-collar workers like Duane; then it hit pink-collar office workers like his wife. The college educated appeared to be keeping a couple of rungs ahead of it. But starting in the late 1990s, real income has been falling sharply for people with college degrees—so far excluding PhDs. You might say that the Pink Slip Club members were a generation and a half behind (or ahead) of the people in Evansville. But it was catching up to them even before the downturn.

So far none of the Pink Slip Four has found a new job. Many employers are loath to hire people who've been out of work for a long time; some say so explicitly in their job postings. But assuming things pick up and businesses begin hiring, what will their jobs look like, feel like, and pay like when the recession recedes?

Chapter Three

INNOVATING THE JOBS AWAY

Skirts, Shirts, and Securities: The Fate of
Small Commissions and Big Bonuses

Ina Bromberg genuinely likes to outfit people. Fashionable women check in each season at the Madison Avenue shop where she works to say, "You know what I like: What have you got for me?"

Trim and well dressed herself, Ina sells petites at the flagship store of a designer brand with several hundred outlets. Even I had heard of the label. But I had to ask its exact place in the fashion hierarchy. "We fall into a niche below Barneys-Bergdorf-Chanel," she explained.

In the course of a twenty-year career at "the Boutique," Ina had been its top-earning national sales associate more than once. Over the years she'd seen her commissions rise and fall according to varied and sometimes confusing formulas. At one point you earned commission only when you sold three or more items to one individual. At other times commission started only after you sold $350 worth of merchandise per hour, averaged daily. But with the recession it became very simple: the company ended commissions.

It also moved the sales staff onto flexible schedules. "On Thursday we are told what our schedule will be for the following week. You can request a change if you have something like a doctor's appointment. But you must do it two weeks before. So they print a schedule for the following week, and they expect everyone to jump to that. But if *you* have a request, it has to be *two* weeks' notice.

"When they told me my new hours that first week, it was down to *ten*. [Ina was already down to twenty-five hours a week by choice, but she still had benefits.] I said, 'Why don't you just lay me off? I can collect unemployment.' And she said, 'No, no, it won't be this way every week.'

"Now, in a way I don't care how many hours I get. My husband is retired, we don't depend on the income, I just like getting out of the house and seeing my regular customers. Here's the problem: There's an article on a fashion Web site about the Boutique. Read the responses. These are by people who worked in the office— probably not anymore. They say that in some of the stores they've taken all the full-time people and made them part-time. And with that there's no more sick days, no more vacation days, no more personal days for *anyone*. They say they're going to do that to all the stores, even New York. In our store we know they've continued the health benefits until March. What will happen after is what we're trying to find out."

"Do they say this is just for the recession?" I asked. "Do they say things will go back to normal when business picks up?"

"Not that I ever heard," Ina answered. "I think—and I've been saying this for a year and a half—I think their *ultimate* goal is to have all part-time salespeople working shifts of four and a half hours. That way they're not responsible for lunch, they have a lot of bodies, they pay no benefits, and it's a constant turnover. This is what I think they want even after the recession because"—here she leaned in for emphasis—*"they haven't stopped hiring people."* She checked to see if I grasped the significance of that.

"When you take on someone for fifteen hours a week, a shift here, a shift there, you certainly don't get someone who's making a profession out of the retail business. Those days are gone. There was a time you came in, you worked full-time, you were sales associate or a desk associate, and you might have thoughts of moving onto the corporate ladder. This is not what you're taking onto staff when you hire people for five-hour shifts.

"My salary has been cut down to probably a fourth . . . No, not cut by a fourth. I make a fourth of what I made a decade ago. But I'm ready to retire. There are a lot of single mothers working in this store. A lot of them are going to school. But this is what some of these people are going to be doing their whole lives. I really feel terrible."

As for Ina herself, she thought she'd probably keep working as long as they give her convenient hours. "I always enjoyed greeting people and speaking to them in a superficial friendly way. That's my outlet for being a little creative, looking at people and thinking what they might wear."

Ina and I spent the rest of our time talking about clothing. She deplored certain of the Boutique's merchandise cutbacks. They had eliminated size 14 petites. "People don't realize that petite is a matter of *proportion*." She just learned that there would be no size 5½ in the fall shoes. "And what could it cost to keep one narrow black belt in a small size in stock to complete an outfit?" To Ina this shortsighted cost cutting eliminated the special features that would bring shoppers back into the Boutique after the recession. Special features like herself, I thought.

I mentioned that a stylish friend once looked me over and said,

"You can get away with those thrift store jackets if you just go into the Boutique and get yourself one pair of black pants that really fit."

"Oh, you look fine," Ina reassured me. "But we can still do black pants." She took my address and promised to send me a notice next time the Boutique had a sale on petite pants.

And if I wanted a good buy on a cashmere sweater to go with the pants, Bendel was closing its clothing department, Ina told me. It would also be a good place to find some unemployed salespeople, she suggested. But I had an appointment with an unemployed securities analyst the next day. I like cashmere, but I wasn't interested enough to stop at the sale on the way to our meeting.

Patrick Dolan, the living cliché of this recession, was a young man who'd been earning somewhere in the low hundreds of thousands just a few years out of college, until his hedge fund shut down abruptly toward the end of 2008. I tried to figure out exactly how much he'd been earning; he countered by explaining how hedge fund compensation works in general.

"The hedge fund industry is bonus-driven. In addition to a base salary, the researcher gets one-third of the profit the company gets from the stocks he recommends. Say they buy a stock at 10 and it goes to 100 by the end of the year—say 110 to make the math easy. The investors made 100. The fund charges 20 percent of that, which is 20. Assuming nothing else, my bonus would be a third of that or $7." (That's $7 times the number of shares purchased by the fund, which is presumably in the tens or hundreds of thousands.)

I doubt that Patrick picked many stocks that went up by 100 points in a calendar year. Still, he'd been a researcher during a few pre-crash years when stocks generally went up. And stock pickers don't give back their bonuses when the stocks they picked later go down. So although he'd worked for a relatively small hedge fund, his bonuses would easily have been in the low six figures.

In any case, Patrick saw no sense to job hunting in other fields where he'd be up against unemployed people with better qualifications. Besides, he loved stock picking, he was good at it, he said, and he intended to stay in an industry where he could make bonuses based on his own skill.

I told him about the saleswoman I just met who loved outfitting people and was skilled at it. But with the recession, everyone at her shop had been moved onto flexible shifts with no commissions. "Her pay is down by three-quarters, she says. And she's worried that things will stay that way even after the recession is over."

"They might," Patrick answered. "Some of the most innovative businesses and business theories have come up during tough times. For example . . ."

I was so nonplussed that I could hardly listen to his examples. I called Ina that evening to tell her about the stock picker who wanted to stay in an industry that awards $100,000-a-year bonuses but thinks that her company may have hit upon an "innovation" by getting rid of sales commissions.

"That was his take? It's innovation?"

"Well, he's young," I said, making an excuse for him. "He knows stock picking; everything else is textbook business school stuff."

"Maybe he'll get 'innovated' in his next job," Ina replied. And our conversation turned from callow youth to cashmere. There wasn't much of a selection left at Bendel, Ina informed me. I'd missed the window of opportunity. But once again, she promised to keep her eye out on my behalf.

Patrick isn't out to *get* people like Ina. It's his profession to spot the practices that would give certain companies an edge. And though he'd been unemployed for nine months, he kept his stock-picking skills honed by looking out for businesses that can keep share prices up in tough times. He had to keep up with innovations, as he'd been asked to name some of his current stock ideas at job interviews.

I asked about labor-cost innovations in his own industry. "Do you think that researchers like you will be offered less pay after the recession?"

"Hedge funds are very small organizations," Patrick told me and cited some as small as three to six people. "If you think about a hedge fund with $500 million in assets, you might have fifteen employees running that. If the fund makes 20 percent return for its investors, the fund itself generated $20 million in fees. So if you had twenty employees, that's $1 million per employee. The owner of the fund will keep a lot of that. But that's still a lot left over."

So although the 30 percent bonus is not an entitlement—"You'll never find that in writing," Patrick said—he thought that hedge funds were not likely to deviate much from the customary. After all, "the people who really generate the profits for the firms are the researchers. And the owners don't want anyone working so close to them to be unhappy."

In the meantime, Patrick and his wife, still employed at another hedge fund, had been making some recession adjustments. "We used to eat out almost every day. Now we're cutting back on things. Like where I used to automatically take a cab, now I might take a subway, little things, things that make sense. I spend a lot of time with my dog. I had a dog walker before. Now I take care of her during the day."

"But it seems like you could probably manage if you never worked again," I said. "I mean, if your wife keeps working."

"Financially, yes; emotionally, no. It's, I just . . ." Patrick wavered, perhaps on the verge of telling me or himself something. "It's just not good for my psyche; it's not good for my . . ." He let that go and abruptly shifted directions.

"Bottom line: here's the way I think about this situation. The economy will come back. Whether it's six months or five years, we will be fine as a country. But if I leave the hedge fund industry and I go work somewhere else, the odds of me getting back into the business are slim to nothing. I love this industry."

I'm sure Patrick endured mental distress that he might have told me about if I'd been more empathetic. But I was too put off by his admiration for the one innovation that worries me the most—making people "contingent."

When we left Ina Bromberg, her commissions at the Boutique had been eliminated and her hours temporarily reduced, but she still had her health insurance. There were rumors that the company was going to get rid of all staff salespeople and end all benefits.

Eventually, the managers called the remaining full-timers into the office and gave them two choices. They could take a severance package and collect unemployment, or they could stay, if they wished, but as part-timers with no benefits. In a way, the Boutique had made U.S. unemployment compensation a part of the company's buyout package. Managers were telling the regular staff, "You go voluntarily, and we'll say we laid you off."

According to Ina, every full-timer took the buyout. The Boutique was now closer to what Ina had postulated as its ideal staff—part-timers with no benefits working flexible, lunchless, four-and-a-half-hour shifts.

Ina had been tense while things were uncertain. Now she sounded not only relieved but satisfied with her own deal.

"So far, knock wood, they let me do what I want about my schedule. I took the whole month of December off. I still enjoy going in to see my old clients who learn my new hours. In a way it was already a semiretirement for me. I didn't depend on the benefits because of my husband. It's also a good deal for college students if someone's paying their tuition. They can come in a couple of evenings or weekends and earn spending money."

Temps

When McDonald's was a new phenomenon, its part-time, minimum-wage jobs were presented as a way for high school students to earn spending money. The company even lobbied Congress to pass a subminimum youth wage as a kind of internship grant for introducing so many American youth to the discipline of work. Now the Boutique has become a good place for college women to earn spending money. With that, another great swath of breadwinner jobs disappears.

Despite Patrick's choice of word, there's nothing terribly innovative about transforming steady jobs into contingent work. Just-in-time staffing has been on the increase since (you guessed it) the 1970s. By 2008, eighteen million people, or one-eighth of the U.S. labor force, were hired as consultants, temps, adjuncts, e-lancers, day workers, or under one of the many other labels used for people who don't have what we used to think of as a regular job. (These statistics come from Steven Greenhouse's *Big Squeeze: Tough Times for the American Worker*.)

At first this hit unskilled workers like those Big Box warehouse-men. But now brain workers like Feldman, of the Pink Slip Club, have increasing difficulty finding staff positions. From low-paid university adjuncts to high-paid mercenary soldiers, skilled work like teaching and assassinating is increasingly handled on a per diem basis by freelancers.

This brings with it a demotion that's often more than just finan-cial.

The nineteenth-century phrase "factory hand" suggested an interchangeable part or tool to be used as needed. There might be an almost familial feeling between the owner and the salaried clerks in the office, but that didn't carry over to the factory floor. You don't treat a *hand* the same way you treat a whole person.

An employer's diminished investment in his contingent workers affects their relationships to each other too. When a permanent employee is sick or injured, the company pays his medical bills, his colleagues sign a get-well card, and a few may visit the hospital. But if a Big Box warehouse temp gets run over by a bus, the com-pany phones the staffing agency to send a new one. The get-well card and the visit are unlikely.

Patrick is probably right that the owner of a hedge fund won't want the half a dozen researchers and perhaps his personal secretary to be alienated from the enterprise. There'll always be a core of real employees in any company. But what if he's also right that an important "innovation" of this recession will leave another large swath of Americans out on the periphery? Aside from being painful to individuals, it's dangerous to a democracy when so many of its citizens are marginal, contingent, and peripheral.

Chapter Four

EVEN BANKERS CAN BE UNEMPLOYED

Sunday Night Fright

Bank workers are no more responsible for financial crashes than autoworkers are for auto crashes, right? I can understand why many Americans were angry when they read about the salaries and bonuses that top bankers awarded themselves right after the bailout. But we'd also seen images of Lehman Brothers employees filing out of the bank carrying cartons of personal belongings. Bankers were recession victims also, and it seemed only fair to interview them too. So I set out to find some.

One Sunday evening around 9:30, I got a call from an unemployed loan officer who had been putting me off. He asked if I could manage lunch the following day.

Russell Wynn is a mellow and amiable-looking man in his late forties. His wife, about a decade younger, still works at the same bank he did. Between her earnings, his severance, and their savings, the couple didn't feel hard-pressed. So far the only thing Russell and his wife had talked about cutting back on were two private school tuitions. But they weren't going to move their children, five and eight, precipitously. They'd see how things worked out.

Russell had been a traditional banker; that is, he made loans. He isn't the man you see for a mortgage, a car loan, or money to upgrade a nail salon. He worked upstairs in middle-market lending. His clients were companies that grossed between $15 million and $750 million a year. Some of his customer relationships spanned almost the entire twenty-six years he'd worked at the bank, he told me.

"Those relationships must have made you very valuable to the bank," I said.

"Unfortunately, my customers had very little need to borrow . . . Right, even before the downturn."

"Businesses didn't need money?" I asked.

"The importers needed seasonal credit," he answered. "But most of my customers didn't need new money. They were awash with cash."

That word "awash" triggered memories of interviews that I'd done with Chase bankers in the mid-1990s. Middle-market bankers like Russell who lent to seafood importers, dental labs, lamp parts manufacturers, and similar concerns had complained that they just couldn't get anyone to take their money. People who lent to large corporations said the same thing. Everyone was "awash" with cash then too.

But salesmen always complain about the territory. I found it hard to believe that local businesses didn't need money. So I'd checked it out by talking to several Chase corporate customers. I told Russell Wynn about an assistant treasurer at ITT whom I spoke to in the mid-1990s.

"This guy said that loan salesmen came around like Fuller Brush men offering interest so low that the loan was the loss leader."

"In a way that's still true," Russell said. His middle-market clients may not have needed loans, he explained, but they paid well for services like currency exchange and pension plan management. "Other areas of the bank delivered those services and booked the fees, but I was the gateway in."

"But you weren't making loans?"

"I had the opportunity to get out of lending at just about the time period you mentioned," Russell recalled, "mid-nineties. Investment banking was open to me, but I felt at the time, well . . ." He tilted his head regretfully. "I just didn't make the move."

To dispel his regrets, it seemed, Russell asked if my food was okay and signaled the waiter for more water. We were in an excellent, unpretentious restaurant that he'd recommended. I always buy meals for my interview subjects; still, Russell had the habits of a gracious host. He also wanted to change the subject.

"So how was your weekend?" I asked.

"Excellent," he replied. "Very ordinary, but the kind of ordinary I like."

I asked for details.

On Saturday he'd taken the children shopping with a stop at the park. On Sunday they visited his wife's mother. "She was embarrassed about having no food in the house, so I went out and bought some hot dogs. Just hot dogs and buns, but cook 'em outside on a grill and everyone is happy. It doesn't have to be summer."

Russell felt fine until he'd put the children to bed on Sunday evening. "They're going to school the next day; my wife is getting ready for work. What do I do Monday? I started to get . . . I don't know if my wife saw how bad it was, but I was . . . not panicked, but frightened, actually frightened, I would have to say."

Now I understood why he'd called me at 9:30.

"My father was retired eighteen years before he died. He only got fragile toward the end. When I visited, we'd argue. Or let's say, we'd leave the discussion with an open point. He would say he'd look it up in the library. But one time I said, 'Wait, I'll Google it.'

"My wife gave me hell on the way home. Why was I taking away a trip to the library—a day with a purpose? After that I always tried to leave him with a couple of things to research. He'd call back with the information, and I thanked him. When he couldn't get to the library anymore, I got him a computer, but he couldn't make the leap.

"My father was a very intelligent man. He handled complicated flow problems they have computer programs for now. But eventually his idea of something to do for the day was to organize his pill case for the week. He was grateful if my mother gave him a job like going through the sock drawer and throwing out singles. Shit, is my wife doing that for me?

"Not knowing what I'm supposed to be doing the next day is the worst part of being unemployed. If I have one significant task that I can check off in the day, like researching before a job interview or writing the thank-you note after—that is much harder than it sounds—then I feel okay."

Of late Russell has been using library computers for his job search. "At first it was embarrassing to admit to myself that I really wanted the walk and the other people around me. I said I needed to go to the library to keep up with various publications and I can't afford to buy them all anymore. But now I admit I just like going to the library. It's more like going to an office. I work in a more concentrated way there."

Russell had been unemployed for five months at that point, he'd been in a backwater of banking, and he was almost fifty. Statistically, things looked bad. But he was a likable man. That was his strong point.

"Your customers obviously appreciated you," I said. "And you knew more about their business than any other outsider. Maybe something more interesting than banking might turn up in one of those businesses," I suggested. "Down the line, I mean, as the economy recovers. Why not put feelers out?"

That got no response.

"Or what about teaching?" I asked. "You seem to be good with children."

Then I thought about all the teachers being laid off. What a stupid suggestion.

"If this goes on much longer," Russell said as a joke before we parted, "I'll need my father's big pill case for something to do and also to hold enough pills to stay calm."

"The Spinning Stuff"

When the U.S. government announced its $700 billion financial bailout, or Troubled Asset Relief Program (TARP), one stated purpose was to enable banks to keep lending. Since then, the president has appealed repeatedly to banks to increase their Main Street lending. Russell Wynn's specialty is Main Street lending. The basic banking function you study in Economics 101 is Main Street lending. Yet Main Street lending had become a backwater well before the recession and remains so today. How can that be?

After I left Russell, I reread my interviews with 1990s Chase bankers with a feeling of déjà vu. Nobody wanted the bankers' money back then either. Everyone was "awash" in cash.

One really hot, prestigious lending area at the time was for M&A (mergers and acquisitions). Chase and other big banks competed to lend multinational corporations the money to buy each other. The borrowed money was used to buy existing assets rather than to expand an enterprise or create a new one. The loans financed a transfer of ownership and left the resulting enterprise with new debt.

There can be many motives for mergers. Mergers and acquisitions are sometimes about limiting competition or about getting ahold of resources or talent. The year 2011 saw a spate of mergers to avoid taxes.

A merger can certainly be part of a plan to grow. But in the 1990s, when companies were competing for declining business, the primary goal of most mergers was to downsize. The M&A loans Chase made in the 1990s were paid back out of the savings from staff cuts. The bigger the cuts, the higher the stock price rose. But with each round of mergers the companies got smaller. I wondered back then how long this no-growth lending could go on.

But the bankers who made the big M&A loans and got the big bonuses often looked down at Russell Wynn's middle-market lending and not only because of the smaller scale. "Loans should be made only to the twenty largest companies in each country," one big lender told me. "To *known* quantities. That way the debt can be chopped up into chunks and sold on the Euro markets." In other words, it could be securitized.

But Russell's mid-market loan applicants were *unknown* quantities—a fish importer in Brooklyn or a dental plate maker in Queens. His job was to investigate their business prospects individually and to lend depositors' money to those he found creditworthy. That's called "intermediation." In textbooks it's the basic function of a bank.

Each of Russell's mid-market borrowers ran a unique business and got a unique "handcrafted" loan for specific purposes. The bank held those unique loans on its books and collected the interest through the life of the loan. But "no one wants an asset on their books," a Chase executive had explained to me in the 1990s. "Liquidity is everything to a money-center bank."

I called Russell back and read those quotations to him. That kind of thinking still applied, he said, and he'd be happy to explain. But first he wanted to thank me. After our lunch he'd called several of his old customers and asked them directly about a job. It hadn't produced any offers yet, but it was the least humiliating networking he'd done so far. "I forgot how down-to-earth those people are."

The experience was so positive that he'd decided to follow through systematically—going through his old client book from *A* to *Z*. He thought he might even drop by some places in person the way he used to when he was their banker. "It's a long shot but . . ."

"But all you need is one," I said, and he agreed.

Russell sounded a lot better than the day we'd met for lunch. Maybe it was because he had a project with tasks to check off each day, maybe because it was ego boosting to talk to people who admired him from his years as their banker, or maybe he felt better because it wasn't a Monday after Sunday evening's existential fright.

I brought Russell's attention back to the criticism of lending to "*un*known quantities" like these businesses whose owners he'd been calling. Russell acknowledged that if you lend to big corporations, you then syndicate or even securitize the debt. At the other end of the loan-size spectrum, you can get small standard loans off your books by bundling them together into securities that you sell to investors. "Subprime mortgage loans are a handy example of that," he pointed out. "They don't have to be good loans, just standard enough to bundle.

"Of course it's exciting," he acknowledged, "to do 100 million in mortgage loans, sell them off the same day, use the money to make more loans that you can also sell immediately, keep spinning the same money around and booking fees each time. That will obviously generate more immediate returns than if you hold the loan till it's paid back. So, yes, that's where the action is.

"But that doesn't mean that the bank doesn't want mid-market loans also," Russell insisted. "They wanted me to make every good loan that I could. The limitation is that my customers don't need new money."

"Even now?" I asked.

"Especially now. Look, factories flip the 'on' switch when orders come in. No one borrows to buy material or equipment, no matter how low the interest rate, unless they know they'll have orders to fill. It's a problem of demand. I was just speaking to a guy that sells . . ." Then he remembered he was talking to a writer. "Your banker is like your doctor or your lawyer. That holds for your ex-banker too.

"So, yes," Russell summarized more generally, "securitization, syndication, derivatives, all the spinning stuff, it's more profitable, more prestigious than plain-vanilla lending. But the bank still wanted me to make as many vanilla loans as I could. The problem is to find businesses that can put the money to use."

Russell left me with a lot to think about. For more than a decade I'd been shaking my head over what he called "the spinning stuff." In February 2011, I heard Phil Angelides, the chairman of the Financial Crisis Inquiry Commission, speak on *The Brian Lehrer Show* on public radio. After a year of investigation, his commission had issued a report on the causes of the financial crisis. Here's part of what he said: "I had spent a lot of my life in the private sector, in finance, and I was stunned by what I learned this year. I was shocked. The extent to which our financial system went from being a system to support the real economy—companies, job creation, wealth creation in this country—to a system that was money making money, financial engineering alone, to the great detriment of the country."

So he too had noticed how much financial activity was about "the spinning stuff." Chairman Angelides gave the impression that if you could slow down the spin and require banks to lend to real businesses for productive purposes, then the economy would recover. But Russell Wynn claims that he'd been free to make all the good middle-market loans he could find; he just couldn't locate qualified borrowers.

The catch is that a bank can't lend unless the borrower can pay back. And that depends on making enough additional profit to cover the principal plus the interest. Normally, that means that a business must be expanding. The borrower must use the bank's money to make and sell more. That in turn depends on buyers. But Americans' wages had been stagnant for forty years. Still, economic life had sputtered along and sometimes accelerated for another two decades despite my fears. A lot of that turned out to depend upon consumer credit.

One scheme to keep people borrowing and spending, the one that triggered the Great Recession, involved lending money to house buyers who didn't earn enough to pay it back. These borrowers were told that they could repay their loans by borrowing yet again against the increasing value of their houses. Their wages might not be going up, but house prices would rise forever.

The trick for the loan originators was to get the mortgages off their own books before the scheme crashed. That involved bundling the mortgages into bonds and selling them off to investors immediately. Some banks hadn't acted fast enough, it seems. Some were even foolish enough to buy the damn things as an investment themselves. When the housing bubble burst, many financial institutions were stuck holding what came to be called toxic assets. I was fortunate enough to meet an unemployed young man who had been right at the center of the mortgage securitization business creating those poisonous bonds.

Creating Value

August Treslow has the gawky charm of a four-year-old Labrador retriever. That's twenty-eight in human years. Gus was, in fact, thirty-four, but he's very youthful. He'd been an unemployed banker for seven months when we met in May 2009.

When I arrived at the restaurant, I found him reading *The Kite Runner*. "I just started reading books a few months ago," he said. "This is the third. A friend recommended *Liar's Poker*. That took a month, but it's not really hard writing."

In addition to reading three books, Gus had worked on a Habitat for Humanity housing project in the Bronx, he'd started to learn the language of his birth country (he was adopted), he was "doing stuff" with his old friends, "not just hanging out with the ones who are unemployed," and he was studying for a test that would give him a certificate as a CFA (chartered financial analyst). "That would prepare me for a job on the sell side."

Before the recession, Gus used his mathematical skills to help create the mortgage-backed securities that were central to the financial crisis and ensuing recession. But he did not, himself, sell these or any other products to investors.

"Are you going out on job interviews?" I asked.

"A couple, but I'm really just studying for the exam. In July, I'll try to interview. Right now I'm just testing the waters. I don't want to be one of those people who makes a full-time job out of finding a job, because the jobs come back when the market comes back and you can't control the market."

In the decade since he'd gotten his MBA, Gus has worked at two major financial institutions, where he had securitized both mortgages and some kinds of corporate loans.

When I asked exactly how he securitized things, Gus took my notebook, reached for a pencil, and covered many pages with diagrams featuring circles inside boxes connected by arrows with the labels MBS, CDS, CDO, CLO, and so on.

Leaving aside the TLAs (three-letter acronyms), this is what I gathered from reviewing the notes. The underlying assets for the bonds Gus created might be 200,000 mortgage loans or some kind of corporate debt. These had been gathered together by the deal manager. The manager was going to sell the right to collect the fruits of these loans to investors. But first they had to be turned into bonds divided into different tranches or slices according to their risk.

Institutions like pension funds that were legally required to be cautious might agree to take a low interest, like 4.5 percent, for the right to collect the first 15 percent of the money that comes in every month. More daring or unregulated investors, like hedge funds, might buy the bottom tranche. They would get 7 percent, perhaps, but they'd collect out of the last 15 percent of the payments that came in on those same 200,000 mortgages.

To make things a little more complicated, some investors were going to be paid out of the interest on the mortgages, some out of the principal, and some out of both. Sometimes groups of bonds were themselves chopped up and bundled together into new securities yet one level further removed from the underlying house mortgages.

Gus's job was to figure out the proper size for each tranche in a way that kept the right balance between the risk and the return. His work was mostly mathematical, but there was some personal interaction too, he told me. Different parties had conflicting interests in having the various tranches smaller or larger, and Gus received many "human inputs" as he worked.

Sometimes the manager of the deal would bring Gus in when he talked to potential investors. "He'd turn to me as the expert to answer specific questions."

But finding buyers wasn't what slowed a bank down. The limiting factor during the heyday of such bonds was getting enough "raw material"—that is, enough mortgages to securitize.

"In business," Gus said as if quoting from one of his MBA courses, "one way of controlling efficiency is to control the pipeline so you can have a steady flow of the raw material. If you're in the copper business, you can buy copper, or you can buy a copper mine. Well, if you were in the mortgage securitization business, you can get a steady flow of mortgages the way everyone else was doing it. Bank of America bought Countrywide, Merrill bought Franklin." These were two big subprime mortgage lenders.

Eventually, a lawyer would incorporate Gus's tranche work and other elements of the deal into a formal contract for investors called an indenture. "It could be a three-hundred-page book," Gus told me.

"My book could be three hundred pages," I said.

"But I'll be paid more," Gus remarked. He knew my kind of writing could be difficult too, he quickly added. But there was a reason for the pay difference. "One person's research might generate hundreds of millions in profits, but what could an academic researcher at a college generate—a million-dollar grant that gets spread over several years, maybe?

"It's not the skills; it's what *value* can be generated from the skills," Gus explained. "It might not be fair, but it's the capitalist system. My work creates a lot of value."

When Gus says his work generates "value," he means profit for shareholders. And since his bank's shareholders retained the profits made from the sale of his tranches in the good years, the shareholders he worked for did indeed come out ahead. By that definition Gus created value.

There was no sense asking him about social value. You can't undo a master's in business administration in one afternoon.

The redeeming thing about Gus is that he didn't complain about his own job loss or any other personal consequences from a system that, in his words, "might not be fair." Gus had an almost spiritual acceptance of capitalist business cycles.

I told him about the hedge fund stock picker who was so determined to stay in his high-bonus industry no matter what.

"A lot of people are determined," Gus responded, "and some will get back. But the truth is a lot of them will leave finance forever. What you have is a pool that gets expanded in good times. In bad times it dries up, gets small. When it expands again, you have a new class of MBAs and undergraduates that can fill in those spaces."

Did that mean that a recent graduate might occupy Gus's old niche when the waters rose again?

Gus wasn't a particularly philosophical fellow, but he seemed, for a moment, to gaze past me into the eons of time in which flowerings and extinctions, recessions and recoveries lay down their layers in the geological record.

"Will the new people eventually be paid as well as you were?" I asked.

"Yeah, I think. In 2000–2001 there was a lot of flak about high-paid analysts doing biased research. Their pay went down for a while, but it went back up because they create *value*.

"There's always cycles. In bad economies the employer has more power. When the economy is good and there's more money around, the employee has more power. When you have people in finance working sixteen, eighteen hours a day plus weekends, if you don't pay them well, you're not going to have finance.

"And what people are learning from this recession is that finance makes the world go around. An employer can take advantage in a bad economy. But if they don't adjust in a good economy, the good people will leave."

"So it finds its balance," I said. My hands moved like balance scales gradually coming to rest in the middle.

"I don't know if there's ever a balance," Gus corrected me dialectically. "It's a continual shift of power from one side to another." His own imaginary scales kept moving through the full range and back.

Gus seemed to find comfort in viewing his own ups and downs as part of the eternal cycle of booms and busts. He was part of economic evolution even if he himself wound up fossilized in a recessionary stratum. There is a grandeur in that view of life, I suppose.

Two years after he lost his bank job, Gus landed a position at the Federal Reserve Bank applying his mathematical skills to risk models.

"The pay is not as good," he told me, "but I have twenty-two days of vacation, nine-hour days, no weekends, and every other Friday off." (I happen to know that the Fed also has a fantastic pension plan, though Gus wasn't thinking that far ahead yet.)

"Which job do you like better?" I asked.

"I liked being part of the pressure before," he answered, "but I also like it that now when I come home, I can go work out or see people."

I couldn't tell whether Gus considered himself back in the pool or fossilized. But I told him that he was the first person I interviewed who had found a permanent, full-time job.

"If you give it more time," he said, "they'll all land somewhere."

The Mystery of the Missing Unemployed Man*

Sizing the tranches of mortgage-backed securities put Gus at the dead center of the financial crisis. But the center of a storm is sometimes calm and quiet. I wanted to talk to one of those high-bonus guys who'd worked a few paces off center, at the turbulent trading desks where Gus's bonds were bought and sold. Traders have a reputation for arrogance, but I suspected I'd find them as innocently enthusiastic as Gus. Alas, the banality of evil makes it difficult to find any villains to interview. Or if they were there, they were too busy to talk to me. Everyone really is just doing his job.

Since mortgage-backed securities had been the downfall of Lehman Brothers, Bear Stearns, Merrill Lynch, the world's largest insurance company, AIG, and many other Wall Street institutions, there had to be plenty of unemployed toxic-asset traders roaming feral on the streets of downtown Manhattan. The "do-you-happen-to-know-anyone-who-worked-at" research method usually works surprisingly well. But I couldn't find a single mortgage-backed securities trader.

Eventually, I phoned Outten & Golden LLP, a law firm representing Lehman Brothers' former employees in a suit for severance pay. The lawyer's job was to make sure they got their fair share of what was left when the bankrupt company's assets were sold off.

I asked partner Jack Raisner if he could possibly inquire among his unemployed plaintiffs for someone who had traded mortgage-backed securities and might be willing to talk to me about how he

* Most of the material in this section appeared first on Tom Engelhardt's elegantly edited Web site TomDispatch.com.

was managing now. "I don't use real names," I assured him. I knew it was a touchy request.

"Most of them were snapped up immediately by Barclays," Mr. Raisner answered.

"What for?"

He represented many other financial clients too, and he thought that the kind of person I was looking for just hadn't remained unemployed very long. Mr. Raisner sounded like an honest and helpful man, but I still thought he might be brushing me off to protect his unemployed clients. How could those toxic-asset traders still be working?

Then I met a banker who confirmed that traders at his company were still busy with asset-backed securities. In fact, he thought he noticed a couple of new chairs at their trading desk. He speculated that "those damn things" had become so complex that the people who put them together were needed to "unwind the bank's positions"—that is, to get them out of the deals. That made sense to me.

Then I saw a column in the *Financial Times* headlined "Strange but True—the Credit Specs [Speculators] Are Back."* The knowledgeable John Dizard reported:

> Even after they've been reviled by talking heads and politicians from here to Ulan Bator, credit default swaps are still a very low-cost way of putting on speculative positions, as long as they still trade. And so, thanks to the Geithner Treasury's policy of reform, rather than dissolution, *CDS trading*

* *Financial Times*, May 27, 2009.

has regained a vampiric strength the real economy still lacks.
(Emphasis mine)

I'm afraid I'm going to have to define a couple of financial terms in order to explain what Dizard found so surprising.

People who buy bonds normally insure them against default. The credit-default swap, CDS, or simply "swap," that Dizard is surprised to see trading again is a special form of insurance.

An insurance company like AIG says to an investor, perhaps a pension fund, "You pay us $7,000 a month, and if you fail to receive the full interest on that mortgage-backed bond for, say two months, then we'll buy the whole bond from you for the $200 million you paid for it."

They couch it in those terms instead of writing a straight insurance policy because insurance is regulated. When AIG sells insurance, it's required to put aside a small amount in reserve in case any of the hazards it insured against occur. But this is a private, custom-written agreement to "swap" a worthless bond for money in case of default.

The first thing bugging the columnist John Dizard is that the U.S. Treasury, under Timothy Geithner, decided to make good on these unregulated non-insurance policies even though AIG had been flouting insurance regulation. The costs of covering these swap obligations were potentially enormous because they involved most of the mortgages in the United States.

But here's something even more shocking. You don't have to own the mortgage bonds to buy the swap/insurance on them.

Any "investor" can go to AIG and say, "You know that Merrill asset-backed bond number 123456? I *too* will pay you $7,000 a month, and if the bond defaults, you'll owe *me* $200 million also."

It's as if any number of people could buy life insurance on the same individual.

If our government was merely going to cover the policies on the original mortgage-backed securities, the maximum payout, though large, was at least calculable. If 80 percent of the mortgages in the United States have been securitized and if a quarter of them eventually default, that's a vast but finite loss.

But any number of people could have bought swaps on the same bonds, related distantly to the same mortgages. So the swap payouts could be many times the value of the real houses. How many times reality will it eventually come to? Two times, ten times, a hundred times? We don't know, because swap trading was (and still is) unregulated. There's no derivatives exchange that, like a stock exchange, keeps track of transactions. (Regulation of this trade is still "pending.")

Not only are swap losses potentially humongous, but the "investment" has nothing to do with anything in the real world. Neither party to these "me too" swaps owns, builds, or finances housing or anything else. Both parties are simply betting on whether a certain group of people will pay their mortgage bills. And, of course, a life insurance policy beneficiary with no relation to the individual insured has an interest in finding the sickest individuals and shortening the life span of those who linger too long. Some of these people were also in a position to create the most unhealthy mortgages and mortgage bonds.

It's the ultimate example of Phil Angelides's "money making money" or Russell Wynn's "spinning stuff." That's why Dizard called it "vampiric." It's something dead feeding on the blood of the living economy.

And according to Dizard, speculators are actively trading these and other debt derivatives again. So my missing unemployed man isn't just cleaning up old messes. He's busy making new ones!

But why are rich people reviving this market and fighting any attempt to regulate it? Aren't they scared of it too? Let me quote Dizard's column once more:

> The credit specs are back. After all, if the dictates of style and tax auditors say you have to go easy on conspicuous consumption, and *if there's no demand for the products of real capital spending*, then you might as well take your cash to the track, or the corner credit default swap dealer. (Emphasis mine again)

"*No demand for the products of real capital spending.*" That means you can't invest your money in a productive business because there aren't enough buyers for the additional products or services they'd make. That doesn't mean there isn't enough need or desire. In economics "demand" means desire backed with money. There's insufficient demand when people aren't earning enough to buy back what they produce.

But in the absence of action in the real world, folks with money have to put it somewhere. The last time a big bookie, AIG, went broke, the U.S. Treasury decided to make good on all its uninsured, unregulated markers. So of course everyone is returning to the track on the assumption that it will do so again. By strengthening the assumption that there's no real risk, the government is fostering what is called moral hazard.

The lawyer representing those Lehman Brothers traders wasn't lying to me. The guys who lost jobs at one off-track betting parlor were immediately snapped up by another. My mysteriously missing unemployed man has been sitting at a trading desk all this time.

Way up on a high floor he's still spinning old asset-backed securities, new securities made of bundles of the defaulted old bonds, swaps to insure them, bets on the swaps, and ever higher, more "derived" financial products.

Meanwhile, many levels of abstraction below, we can make out tiny houses with ant-sized people at the windows and barely visible "For Sale" signs on the lawns. Those are the "assets" these asset-backed securities are ultimately backed by. As we get closer, we can see that the ants are agitated. For though the highest-level lenders were relieved of their risks, the ground-level borrowers still owe as much as ever. In many cases it's more than they can pay.

When I contacted people who faced recession-related home loss, I found that I could understand the mortgage crisis best by arranging their stories in order of their escalating difficulties. So we'll start with someone who merely fell behind and work our way up (or down) to foreclosure and eviction.

II: OUR HOMES

Chapter Five

SHOW ME THE MORTGAGE

Buying Them Time

At the start of the Great Recession, I heard that you could stop an eviction by demanding to see the mortgage. The notion gained currency because of the way that mortgages passed from owner to owner until they were bundled by the tens or even hundreds of thousands into mortgage-backed securities. Some investors collected only the principal payments from these mortgages, others only the interest payments. So who holds the mortgages themselves?

According to instant urban lore, the original mortgages were often misfiled, physically lost, or impossible to tie to particular investors. So when they knock on the door to evict you, you say, "Howdy, Sheriff. I'm a law-abiding citizen, but I don't think those people own this house. I'll leave as soon as you *show me the mortgage.*"

I'd heard it from community organizers; I'd heard it from lawyers; I'd even heard a congresswoman instruct her constituents, on network television, to demand to see the mortgage when they come to take your house. I hadn't heard of anyone who succeeded. As a matter of fact, I hadn't located anyone who actually tried it. That remained true even after the robo-signing scandal of 2010 exposed

the fact that clerks at mortgage companies signed hundreds of foreclosure papers a day without checking the original mortgage documents whose existence and terms they swore to. But way before
that scandal I heard about a judge who seemed to be saying something similar to "show me the mortgage" in his courtroom.

The housing bust was relatively mild in New York City, but
from its beginning the Brooklyn judge Arthur M. Schack developed a reputation for standing up to banks and thwarting foreclosures. In his 2007 decision in *Deutsche Bank National Trust
Company v. Castellanos*, he quoted George Bailey (Jimmy Stewart)
confronting the evil banker Mr. Potter (Lionel Barrymore) of *It's
a Wonderful Life*:

> Do you know how long it takes a workingman to save five
> thousand dollars? Just remember this, Mr. Potter, that this
> rabble you're talking about . . . they do most of the working
> and paying and living and dying in this community. Well, is
> it too much to have them work and pay and live and die in a
> couple of decent rooms and a bath?

Schack had been a lawyer for the Baseball Players Association—
"I represented millionaires against billionaires"—before he became
a Kings County Supreme Court judge. At five feet five inches and
two hundred pounds, he looked, on the bench, like one of those
Russian stacking dolls. "The third or fourth doll in," I thought as
I followed behind him into his chambers.

By the time I met him in 2009, more than thirty of Judge
Schack's decisions were linked to on a Web site called the Home
Equity Theft Reporter. So I was ready to hear some radical talk
about reversing that theft. But the most Judge Schack would say

to me about his judicial philosophy was "I try to buy the little guy some time."

Here's how he did that.

In Florida the legislature set up special "rocket docket" foreclosure courts, hiring retired judges to get through the backlog. At the time, courts in Fort Myers, Florida, were handling a thousand foreclosure actions a day. Most of them received as much judicial time as it took to apply a stamp or a signature where the bank needed it. (Fewer than half the states in the Union even require a judicial signature to foreclose. New York and Florida are among the states that do.)

When homeowners actually appeared in court, one Fort Myers judge permitted them to answer only two questions: "Are you living in the home?" "Are you current on your mortgage?"

Brooklyn's housing caseload wasn't nearly as high. Still, foreclosures accounted for about 30 percent of the Kings County Supreme Court's docket. That didn't stop the judge from applying an unusual procedure. When Judge Schack gets a foreclosure application, he betrays his bias toward the little guy by actually reading it. If it's full of errors, he denies the foreclosure until the papers are cleaned up.

The chubby judge swiveled toward the teetering piles of documents on his windowsill and pulled out three examples while somehow leaving the stacks standing.

"This one . . ." He handed me papers on a ghetto walk-up that had been foreclosed. "But no one from the bank told the tenants, so the former landlord kept showing up for over a year to collect the rent."

The most recent tenant had found her apartment on Craigslist, the judge told me. "She paid $3,000—one month's rent and a month's security—to a scam artist." For the tenants' sake, Judge Schack delayed clearing the building for ninety days.

The second case Judge Schack pulled out concerned a man named Jonas Earl who lived on a block of single-family houses near my old high school, James Madison in Flatbush. The neighborhood was now black and Russian and still solidly middle-middle class. In 2006, Earl had taken out a $375,000 loan against his house with Contour Mortgage Corporation, which sold his note to a loan company called Option One. (Hold on to that name.)

Option One passed Earl's debt along to other financial institutions until it finally became part of the asset-backed certificate 2006-OPT4, managed by Deutsche Bank. But Judge Schack (remember, he actually reads these papers) noticed that the first transfer in the chain occurred *a day before* Earl signed for his loan. "Nonexistent mortgages and notes are incapable of assignment," the judge said, throwing the case out "with prejudice."

"Does that mean he gets to keep the house," I asked, "and they'd just be out that cash?"

Judge Schack laughed, perhaps at the way I'd suddenly reversed sides at the idea of a real "little guy" walking away with 375,000 real dollars. But all the judge would say about his decision was "I bought him some time."

"But what if Contour and Option One can't find the correctly dated paperwork?" And I told him about the myth I still cherished: "The sheriff comes to Earl's door, and he says, 'Of course, sir, but first show me the note I signed.'"

"Like the silent movies," the judge said, kidding me. "*Perils of Pauline.* The guy with the black mustache forecloses on the mortgage and ties her to the railroad track, but our hero comes along and . . ."

"Yes," I had to admit. That's what I'd hoped was going on in his courtroom.

Judge Schack had never heard of any case where they "lost" the mortgage. He explained that all mortgages are registered immediately by the block and lot. "Things may get messy as the debt passes from brokers to banks to investor trusts and back to the bank or some mortgage servicer to handle. Then you might sometimes find that bank X doesn't own it but bank Y does. It can get murky, that's the word you should use, 'murky.' But in New York you need a judge to approve a foreclosure, so they have to establish who owns it *before* the sheriff comes to your door."

Judge Schack's "little guy" decisions merely required that the banks establish things properly.

"Here's a good one . . ." The final decision Schack showed me opened with a quotation from Gretchen Morgenson in the *New York Times* Sunday business section:

It's dispiriting indeed to watch the United States financial system, supposedly the envy of the world, being taken to its knees. But that's the show we're watching, brought to you by somnambulant regulators, greedy bank executives and incompetent corporate directors.

Schack had extended Morgenson's "show" metaphor in the foreclosure action against Susana Elsemeer:

The show we're watching in this . . . action features a possible incestuous relationship between HSBC BANK USA, NATIONAL ASSOCIATION, AS INDENTURE TRUSTEE FOR THE REGISTERED NOTE HOLDERS

OF RENAISSANCE HOME EQUITY LOAN TRUST 2006-4 (HSBC), Ocwen Loan Servicing (OCWEN), Delta Funding Corporation (DELTA) and Mortgage Electronic Registration Systems, Inc. (MERS) that might also include Goldman Sachs and Deutsche Bank.

Judge Schack noted in his decision that the address of the plaintiff, HSBC, is care of the large mortgage servicer Ocwen at 1661 Worthington Road, suite 100, in West Palm Beach, Florida, while the mortgage assignment was executed by one Scott Anderson, vice president of MERS, who gives his address as 1661 Worthington Road, suite 100. The judge, who not only reads the documents but remembers them, went on to cite previous foreclosure requests in which both Deutsche Bank and a Goldman Sachs real estate subsidiary were also said to be housed in the same suite 100. On one document Scott Anderson swore that he was HSBC's servicing agent, and two days later he swore that he was a vice president of MERS.

"Did Mr. Anderson change his employer between June 13th and June 15th?" Judge Schack asked. "The Court is concerned that there may be fraud on the part of HSBC, or at least malfeasance."

So before the Elsemeer foreclosure could go forward, Judge Schack demanded to see "an affidavit from Scott Anderson clarifying his employment history for the past three years . . . and an affidavit by an officer of HSBC explaining why HSBC purchased a nonperforming loan from Delta Funding Corporation, and why HSBC, OCWEN, MERS, Deutsche Bank and Goldman Sachs all share office space in Suite 100."

In a general way, I could give him some of the answers myself. A mortgage servicer is delegated by the mortgage owner (which may be a bank or an investor group) to handle collections and other contacts with the homeowner. Ocwen may have serviced some mortgages for all the banks the decision mentions. So it might be convenient for them to use Ocwen's address for certain mortgage-related dealings.

MERS is a private registry set up in 1995 by Fannie Mae, Freddie Mac, and other major lenders to keep track of mortgages as they change hands in the Grand Allamande of securitization. One of MERS's primary functions is to thwart my show-me-the-mortgage scenario through careful record keeping. But as we learned in the fallout of the robo-signing scandal, some twenty thousand people like Ocwen's Scott Anderson, at mortgage companies around the country, were allowed to log in to the MERS computerized mortgage registry and make changes. In the middle of a gold rush this procedure for registering claims invites error at the very least.

The mortgage of Susana Elsemeer of Decatur Street in Brooklyn may have passed through many of Scott Anderson's "employers" on its way to being lumped with thousands of others into Renaissance Home Equity Loan Trust 2006-4. Every step from originating this mortgage to foreclosing may have been sloppy and deliberately obfuscated, but was it any more malfeasant than the rest of the U.S. mortgage system? Does the judge really believe there's fraud afoot in suite 100?

"If you're going to take away someone's house," says Judge Schack, "it better be legal and correct."

He handed me a copy of the Elsemeer decision, but I couldn't extract the human story from the legalese, so I peppered him with questions. "No," he told me, he'd never gotten that employment history from Scott Anderson. "Yes," any corrected foreclosure papers would have to come back to him if the company had tried to straighten it out. That made it likely that the matter had been settled out of court.

"So how did it end? Who got the house?"

When he shrugs, Judge Schack looks even more like one of those Russian dolls. But that was the only response he could make. All he can tell me about Susana Elsemeer and her co-defendant, Samuel Elsemeer, is "I bought them some time."

"This Is My Tara"

I drove down the shopping street nearest the Elsemeer home looking for a supermarket, but all I saw were a couple of dismal food marts. A peeling three-story building with an empty storefront bore the sign "For Sale $1,000 Down, No Closing Cost."

But as soon as we turned onto Decatur, we were on a tree-lined block of nineteenth-century Brooklyn. Six-Sixty was one of the most elegant town houses on the street.

No one answered on the parlor floor, but a male head emerged from the below-street-level door and told me that Susana Elsemeer was sleeping. I asked if I could speak to the co-owner, Samuel Elsemeer. "That's me," he said. "Susana is my mother."

Samuel, a large young black man, made me comfortable in the kitchen on the ground floor, or "servants" floor, and went to check on his mother. "She'll be right down," he reported. Susana Elsemeer soon scurried in, lively as a squirrel. At the mention of Judge Schack's name, she seemed to do a delighted little skip-hop.

Eager to be interviewed, Susana emphatically said, "I've lived in this house all my life," giving me time to copy it down. But she quickly corrected the facile sound bite. "Well, I traveled a little, and I was married a little. But I've lived in this house"—she did the calculations—"maybe fifty of my fifty-nine years."

Her parents bought the house on the GI Bill in 1951, then raised their family and died there. At that time Susana was back living on Decatur Street with little Samuel. She had to buy her brother's and sister's shares of the house if she wanted to stay.

"That was only fair," she pointed out. Still, she couldn't help remembering, "I did all the shoveling snow and the heating and that stuff while their names were still on the title." She had also helped pay off her parents' mortgage from her earnings as a free-lance typist when Samuel was a toddler.

"So I took out a mortgage loan to pay them off, and I used the leftover to replace all the windows. Then there was a water main break—that cost me $6,000 . . . later roofing, and then . . ." According to the foreclosure papers, there was a consolidated debt of $463,817.64 when Susana Elsemeer missed a payment in 2007.

By then she was working as a school secretary and boarding foreign youngsters from a Manhattan language school to pay the mortgage. "Because I had a young man in the home, I chose to host young guys—from seventeen to twenty-five or so is what they sent. Samuel would take them out in the mornings to the subway and point them in the right direction. He still gets birthday cards from one of the French kids that we entertained.

"It was very good money."

"How much?" I asked.

"One eighty-five a week for a room upstairs and two meals."

"Wait, you served breakfasts, worked full-time, and then cooked dinner every single night for a crowd of students?!"

"Well, I'm a big cooker, Samuel will tell you. Some things I don't know how to make small."

"Still," I said, remembering my own single parenthood, "some nights you just want to eat a spoonful of peanut butter and sit there and stare."

"Especially when I was the suspensions secretary at the high school. I was stressed, stressed, stressed. But in the beginning Samuel helped me. If I was tired, I put a good face on it for the kids.

"Then Samuel went off to the Job Corps to learn a trade and get his GED, and then I had the knee surgery, and then the recession came and the students dried up. First it got sporadic, but after Lehman Brothers and all that craziness the bottom dropped out. So at that point in time I was dealing with empty-nest syndrome *and* empty-pocket syndrome."

That's when Susana missed a payment and began the process of negotiating a series of forbearance agreements with her mortgage servicer. A forbearance agreement allows a debtor to pay a lesser amount and defer the rest, plus interest, to an agreed later time.

"What was it like dealing with Ocwen?" I asked.

"Ocwen?" Angst came into her voice. "I was working at a high-stress job; I was taking an Access-a-Ride back and forth to Manhattan, sometimes traveling four hours a day. Then you get home and call Ocwen, and it says, 'The waiting time will be an hour and a half.'"

"They actually *said* an hour and a half?" I asked dubiously.

"Do you remember that, Samuel? They would say, 'Waiting time two hours,' 'Waiting time two hours forty minutes.' So you take your food upstairs and sit at the phone after work; you sit on the weekends. I called for months, and they would put me in a queue."

"You must have gotten through to somebody, sometime?" I said.

"Yes, and you know what happened. I'll never forget that. I waited and I got to someone in Indian customer service, and he said he was going to transfer me to somebody else, and I said to him, 'Please don't put me back in that queue again.' I said to him, 'I have waited so long.' I said, '*Please*, are you *sure* you're going to connect me to a person?' And he put me right back in the queue."

"This was at a time when you were going into another default?"

"Yes. There was one time that I even had a check that sat in my dresser and I couldn't get in touch with anyone."

"So how did you . . . ?"

"I wrote to the New York State Banking Department and—"

"You needed the New York State Banking Department to contact your own mortgage company?"

"What I found out is you don't talk to customer service. What I found out is you've got to get through to the people who have the authority to make these decisions, and they did that. So this was a learning process."

"That must have felt terrible," I said stupidly.

"I felt like David facing Goliath, only I had no rock and I had no slingshot and I wouldn't have known what to do with it if I had it. I felt small, powerless, put-upon, ignored—all of those good things.

"But Samuel will tell you, I've stood and I've fought for this house for a long time. I'm smart and I'm educated, in certain ways, and if I'm determined to find something out, you're not going to keep it away from me. I contacted the New York State Banking Department, and then the office of the ombudsman from Ocwen called me, and we worked out a forbearance agreement.

"But it was a bad agreement because at that point in time I didn't understand the difference between a forbearance and a loan modification." A forbearance agreement temporarily lowers a monthly payment, but you still owe all of your remaining mortgage plus additional interest. A modification permanently changes the terms of the mortgage by lowering either the interest rate or, less frequently, the principal that's owed. "Besides, I just wasn't financially stabilized at that point. When I had the students, I could pay it; when I didn't have the students, I couldn't pay it. This was one of my darkest points. I was in an agreement, but I couldn't keep it."

"So what did you do?"

"I stayed awake nights and I worried and I cried and I prayed and I did all that stuff. I thought about taking in foster children. I thought maybe it would be nice to have some older girls. You know, be a role model, a power woman. But I'm getting older. I mean, the interaction with the students was intense. You can imagine young girls and their problems and dramas. I said, 'I'm going to have to do something; I'm going to have to declare bankruptcy. Let me first start out with a consumer credit counseling service.'

"I was in such a state, I was so embarrassed. You know how they tell you to bring your bills. I had paper all over this place, and all I could do is take everything in a shopping bag. The lady would ask to see something, and I would just pull stuff out. I said, 'I'm not usually like this; I'm a secretary. I work with paper all day long.'

"Finally, she looked at the things and she said, 'You're asking for the wrong thing. This is not going to work. You have to go back and tell them that you need a loan *modification*.'

"I got to be the queen of modifications and forbearances. I was in two forbearance agreements that I couldn't keep, then a modification.

"Then one August morning—schools were closed for the summer, and I was sitting upstairs worrying—a miracle came through the mailbox.

"At that point in time I was current on my latest forbearance agreement, so I thought I was safe for another month. What I didn't know until aftersight is just because I was in an agreement didn't mean I was *safe*, because meanwhile they were going ahead with foreclosure, and rightly so." Banks in modification negotiations reserve the right to continue with foreclosure and often go ahead. "So these two things were going along parallel with each other, and then out of the blue his decision came."

Susana Elsemeer may not have heard about the bank's foreclosure petition, but she saw immediately that Judge Schack's answer to it bought her time. But time to do what?

"It took *two* miracles. If Judge Schack had said 'fine' and rubber-stamped it, everything would have been different. And the second miracle—maybe it was not the *best* of miracles . . ." Susana stopped herself short and directed her voice upward. "I'm sorry, God, I shouldn't have said that." Then she turned back to explain the lesser miracle to me.

"What happened is, when I first got working, I didn't officially work for the city. I officially joined the Department of Education in 1994. I wasn't aware for a couple of years that I could change my pension tier. Tier one is the old-timers, and naturally they have the best deal. I put in for a conversion, which is, I worked for the city for fourteen years, but now I'd be given credit, in certain ways, for twenty years. It takes a long time, but sometime during that summer they must have juggled the numbers. In the fall I got a statement. I barely had any money because, naturally, I'd taken out loans on my pension all along. But suddenly my pension—not the 401(k) part, but the other part—had an available loan of like $11,000. At that point I knew for certain, *I can manage.*

"You know something. To this day, and I am a woman of faith, to this day I don't know why I got sent a copy of that decision. It didn't make any sense at first, because I didn't know I was in foreclosure. But I read those first couple of paragraphs, and I laughed myself to death. All the problems I had with Ocwen seemed to be distilled in those paragraphs. I just sat down, I called up my girlfriend, and we laughed and laughed and laughed and laughed because she knew everything that was going on with me and Ocwen. She has a little kid's voice and she said, 'He certainly seemed angry with them.' And I said to her, 'Let me tell you something, I don't know what this is all about,' I said, 'but there's something good in it for me because they were the bad guys and he just chased them all back to this little room. All those big banks in one little room.' I was just so tickled."

I asked Susana if it had felt different to negotiate with Ocwen once she had the judge's decision behind her. I expected her to crow about how fiercely she bargained once she had a rock for her slingshot. But instead her whole body seemed to sigh.

"I couldn't do it," she said apologetically. "I couldn't start the telephone calls. I couldn't start with the ombudsman's office." She appealed for my understanding. "I was seriously considering bankruptcy. I was ready to have a nervous breakdown. Emotionally, I couldn't talk to Ocwen again. I just couldn't. I wanted someone to do it for me.

"So this last time I did some research on loan modification companies." She must have seen my dismay. The newspapers were full of stories about crooked and useless modification schemes, and I would soon meet people who fell for them.

"My friend who's a realtor said, 'Don't do it, don't pay anyone.' But no one is walking around in your shoes. I did good research, and I found a company called Amerihope. They have a Web site. I paid them $1,200 in installments.

"They told me that Ocwen was getting ready to foreclose again in court. I guess they had gotten it together, got their papers correct. I would have had to show up myself; I would have had to retain a lawyer for a lot more money than $1,200. These people went in, and they got me the last agreement, which I am getting ready now to make the third payment on. I got a letter in the mail saying that the charges against me, against the house and what not, they've been dropped." Late fees and other charges connected with mortgage delinquencies can be flabbergasting. "I have the letter upstairs on my printer. And that's how the last agreement happened.

"And now that I have respectable, steady money coming in from three roomers and I had the money from the pension for a new down payment, I could make a payment plan that I can keep."

Susana's new monthly payment of $2,900 is actually higher than some earlier negotiated payments, but it's doable as long as she keeps collecting rent from the three single adult roomers that her friend in real estate helped her find. But the recession was dragging on. What if one of them loses a job? I wondered. Where would Susana find another miraculous cache of capital after borrowing the maximum from her pension? And how will she ever be able to retire?

Susana and Samuel saw me out.

"It's too gorgeous," I said, breathing the air on Decatur Street. "It's going to be gentrified."

"Hey, they're jogging with dogs already," Susana responded. "I stood here this spring with my next-door neighbor—he's been here like forever—and we saw them jogging with these little dogs, it's like, 'The pit bulls are going and the poodles are coming in.' I've said to Samuel, someday he'll be able to demand a million for this house."

"So his only way to enjoy the house may be to sell it?" I suggested.

"We're disputing with that now. I'm getting tired of the cold weather. But we're not sure the neighborhood is gonna change quickly enough. I tell Samuel if he *does* get into those unions [Samuel was up for an apprenticeship program] and he's making the money, then I'll go get a little place somewhere where it's warm and then come back and forth and maybe he'll have a family and maybe not.

"But it's gotten so shabby." She turned to look at the house. "The staircases need carpets, I want to redo the outside. Not with that stuff they used across the street." She points to a house with modern siding. "My dream is one of these days I'll be able to restore it to the way it was. Like on *This Old House*, the one they did on Sterling Place"—a Brooklyn town house that had had a televised restoration.

"Anybody who knows me knows two things," Susana said, summing up. "They know Samuel, and they know this house. That's my life."

"It's gorgeous," says Samuel.

"And we love it," says his mother.

The tiny black woman sweeps her arm back toward the Brooklyn town house and says, only half joking, "This is my Tara, and I swear I'll never be hungry again."

Susana Elsemeer and I are small, wisecracking, middle-aged women with almost the same Brooklyn accents. We were both single parents, and we both spent our prime years managing the family's finances alone. The big difference between our two financial systems was savings—or capital.

Before my daughter was born, I had put away about $30,000 from a play I wrote. It was easy to save since I earned the money all at once. My system from then on was to put all my book advances (also earned all at once) in the bank and spend them as slowly as possible. I never had much more than $30,000 during my single years, but I was always *ahead of the game.*

When my daughter broke a tooth, I paid cash; when Susana's house broke a water main, she borrowed. That meant that the $6,000 repair cost her $10,000 or $12,000 or more as she paid it off. Meanwhile, she had that much less equity in the house.

Susana borrowed on her parents' house in order first to buy and then to maintain it. Then she borrowed from her pension (and not for the first time) in order to put enough cash back into the house to get a mortgage payment she could afford. She's already hollowed out her two most obvious sources of savings, her house and her pension. How will Susana ever get *ahead of the game?*

What about saving out of her wages?

Even cheap as I am, I'm not sure I could have come up with a budget that would have allowed a school secretary to set aside enough cash to cover a mortgage of close to $3,000 a month in so deep a recession.

Susana had deliberately rented through a foreign school so she wouldn't be dependent upon more economically insecure local renters, she'd told me. Though that is what she has now. But she considers them stable since her friend the realtor helped her to find them. Susana herself never mentioned being black or living in a black neighborhood as an economic problem. Still, she'd "diversified" in a manner that would leave her less vulnerable to black or even U.S. unemployment. But she hadn't prepared for a global recession.

When it came, the Elsemeer finances were precarious enough

that despite a good union job (formerly known as a regular job) it took two miracles—a windfall of time plus a windfall of credit—for this single earner to save her house. But save it she did. And though she's fallen behind a time or two since, she will keep it, I'm sure.

I was still hoping to find someone who got his house free and clear because the bank couldn't produce all the pieces of the sliced-and-diced mortgage. Frankly, I was a little disappointed that Susana hadn't used Judge Schack's decision to say, "Show me the mortgage—or at least, give me a lower interest rate." But in fact, I had just seen the happiest housing outcome I ever would.

I wish I'd taken a picture of Susana and Samuel Elsemeer waving from their town house steps. Judge Schack would love to see it. By the way, they asked me to convey their profound gratitude.

Chapter Six

BUBBLE BIRTH CONTROL

With This Debt I Do Thee Wed

A woman I know was worried about a relative with large student loans. I arranged to phone the young man in Minneapolis. Actually, he did the calling over his Skype, and though I had no video camera myself, I answered his ring and suddenly beheld the head and shoulders of a moonfaced man in his thirties with a modest and appealing smile.

Karsten Lind teaches theater in a private high school; his wife teaches music. Together they earn about $100,000 a year, and they enjoy what they do. They must be good at it too, because neither of them has been out of work during the course of this recession. To make life even sweeter, they have a toddler that they both adore.

In the 1990s, Karsten did just what young people were encouraged to do: he "invested in himself." In the course of four years of undergraduate and one year of grad school, he amassed a BA, an MFA, and $85,000 in student loans.

But he'd paid that down to $45,000 during his first teaching job. It was at a boarding school where he had virtually no living expenses. Soon his teaching salary went up, but he had household expenses and dropped his student loan payments down to $500 a month. At that rate they'll be paid off in seventeen years.

It irks Karsten when he's visited by friends from other countries who graduate debt-free and can take a year off to explore the world. It also bothers him that while the Fed keeps interest rates low, he still pays 8.25 percent on his loan. "I'm basically paying twice as much as current students for a product that is guaranteed by the government. What a deal for the banks." Unlike most other loans, student loans are not allowed to be refinanced and can't be discharged in bankruptcy. "Think if you could lend your money out at 8.25 percent and know that unless the U.S. government goes bankrupt, you're not going to lose a thing."

A few years earlier Congress considered legislation that would allow student loans to be refinanced like mortgage and other loans, without losing their government guarantees. The proposal was lobbied away by lenders. So student borrowers of Karsten's vintage were paying up to 8.5 percent while banks got their funds at less than .5 percent. I can see why that annoys him.

Still, $500 a month on a $50,000-a-year job might be regarded as a modest agent's fee. How sad to think of one's education in such a mercenary way. Still, to me, Karsten's debt seemed manageable.

Then he happened to mention something about his house in Washington, D.C. "Wait, aren't you calling from Minneapolis?"

That's when I learned that the couple had done something else normal for young families. Once they were "occupationally settled," Karsten and Anita bought a house.

"We were both teaching in D.C. private schools in June 2006. We were both making somewhere in the fifties at that point, so a little over $100,000 combined. But we had no idea what we could afford. So before we started house hunting, we went to Countrywide—one of those big loan companies that caused all these problems.

"The mortgage broker took down our information, went through all their rigmarole, and said we could borrow $475,000. Which, I mean, in retrospect, it's preposterous.

"We didn't have a real estate agent at the time, so the mortgage broker said, 'Oh, I have a really close friend who is a great agent. Let me give her your name.'" (In many ways Karsten is as innocent as his appealing smile.) "The agent took us around the Washington area and did not show us a single house under $400,000.

"We told her that we wanted to pay $250,000, and she showed us one that was $399,000. But it got into a bidding war and sold for $426,000. Basically, she just wanted to show us that $400,000 was a normal price.

"Anyway, I found a listing myself online just outside of the city. It was listed at 299. I went myself, I looked around and called Anita and I said, 'I think we should get it inspected and put in an offer.' One of the things the realtor didn't like about that house was that they were only offering 1.5 percent commission to the buying agent. She basically refused to write a contract unless we upped that to 2.5 percent, which is why we bought a $299,000 house for $301,500.

"So basically we bought a house for $300,000 that had sold ten years earlier for $45,000 and was in need of a lot of work."

Over the next five years Karsten and Anita put in the work, paint, lumber, and love that made them happy with their house. But they began to be unhappy with their jobs. And when their daughter was born, they realized that they'd rather raise their child somewhere else.

"We saw when we started job hunting that it was pretty much impossible for two performing arts teachers to find work at the same time in the same city." But when Anita got a permanent job in Minneapolis and Karsten was offered a one-year sabbatical replacement spot, "We committed to coming to Minneapolis and went to put the house on the market."

That's when they grasped what had been going on in the outside world while they were busy teaching and starting a family.

"We had an agent over; he was actually the selling agent when we bought the house. He came, looked at all the upgrades we made, and said, 'There's no chance you're going to get more than $200,000 for this.'

"Funny thing," Karsten observed, "the Washington area didn't get hit that hard in the crash. There are parts of Montgomery and Fairfax Counties that are now back above their 2006 high. But we had bought in a transitional neighborhood. It's a really nice block with lovely neighbors and an organic co-op. But once a year there was a shooting on a block behind our house."

"It didn't transition fast enough?" I asked.

"It took a dive. Look it up if you like. The zip code is _____. In the six months before we went to sell, not a single house in that zip code had sold that wasn't either a foreclosure or a short sale." In a short sale you sell a house for below the mortgage debt with the bank's agreement that it will accept the sum you get as full payment. Short sales are notoriously difficult to negotiate with banks.

At that moment the Linds had a buyer who'd agreed to pay $115,000 for the house, but his commitment ran out in three weeks. They were waiting for approval from two banks that jointly held the mortgages. They had tentative approval from one.

"While we're waiting, we're paying mortgage, utilities, insurance, taxes in D.C., which comes to $3,000, and $1,100 rent in Minneapolis and going further into debt each month."

"Who's lending you all that money?" I asked.

"Credit cards," he answered.

"Oh," I said.

Karsten's expression acknowledged the dubiousness of that recourse. The couple already had $30,000 in credit card debt. "Twelve or 13 percent, I think," Karsten said in answer to my query about his interest rate. He called off camera to confirm those numbers with his wife. But no matter how high the interest it was imperative, they felt, that they keep paying on the D.C. house.

"Our lawyer says this short sale, by itself, will knock about 100 points off our credit scores—between 100 and 150. If you also don't pay your mortgage during the six months leading up to your short sale, that knocks another 200 points off your credit. So if we stopped paying our mortgage, we'd be looking at a 300-point ding in our credit, which would decimate our chance of ever getting another mortgage. So we're doing our best to keep paying till our short sale is approved, and we'll only take about a 100-point ding."

Good Lord, this young couple is sacrificing not to keep a roof over their child's head but to keep open the *possibility* of buying another roof. They're renting a four-bedroom house in Minneapolis for less than half of what it cost them to be "owners"—owners who paid $36,000 a year for six years and can hope for no gain from the sale of their property beyond the possibility of emerging without a huge debt.

The whole thing was so depressing that by some mutual impulse we segued from mortgages to a subject that delights us both: musical theater. Karsten told me with enthusiasm about shows he'd done with his students. We talked with pleasure about musicals that we liked because they're also good plays. Karsten is one of those generous souls who frankly acknowledges that he couldn't make it in the professional theater world yet has not soured on either theater or himself.

"So let me get this straight," I said, bringing us back to the couple's finances. "You're paying $3,000 a month on a house you're not living in, $1,100 a month on the place you're renting, $500 a month on your student loans, $1,600 a month for day care, and your credit card minimum is?"

Their minimum was $650, Karsten told me. "We try to pay $1,000 a month when we can."

"So you must be living a bit less affluently than two teachers usually do," I ventured.

"We have mostly cast-off Goodwill furniture; we would never go out and spend a thousand dollars on anything. My wife is an amazing pianist; I would love for her to have a great piano. But we just can't do that.

"There are so many people," Karsten explained earnestly, "who can't afford to buy the luxuries that their parents could, or things that people without that mass of debt can afford."

"By the way," I asked, "do your own parents understand how difficult things are these days? Or do they think, 'Those kids made bad choices'?"

"I think my parents believe that we made the right decisions for where we were. I don't think they're judgmental about that. But, God, they would *love* for us to have another child. As would we. *I would love for Eva to have a sibling!* And we still may if we can get rid of this house. But, you know, if it takes another two or three years for us to get back on our feet financially, that may not be a possibility."

"You mean the window of opportunity will have closed?"

"In a way that's the price we pay," Karsten says.

"The price you pay for what, though?"

"The price we pay for having been part of a burst of a bubble and for having bought into something that seemed right but that"—he pauses—"was wrong."

When the housing boom suddenly went bust, about one-quarter of American mortgage borrowers were left with "negative equity," meaning that like Karsten and Anita they'd wind up owing the bank if they sold their houses. Economists worried that that would leave the traditionally flexible American labor force less mobile. People who'd have to lay out $200,000 or go on paying $3,000 a month in order to move might decide to stay put. The other option, if the job was good enough and the mortgage bad enough, was to simply walk away. A lot of people were doing that.

But the Linds had the daring (or naïveté) to move for work and assume that they could work it out with the bank. Maybe they will. But in their short sale two lending banks have to agree to take a loss. We'll soon meet people whose bank negotiations stretched out for a year and a half. I wonder how long the Linds will keep paying on two residences if delays arise?

Chapter Seven

UNDERWATER AND UP THE CREEK

Mortgage Mania

Susana Elsemeer couldn't pay her mortgage when she lost her renters, and Karsten Lind couldn't sell when the bust put his house underwater. Still, New York and the D.C. area were only moderately affected by the mortgage crisis.

California was the Wild West of mortgage innovation. Nine out of the top ten subprime lenders were based in California before the crash, and so were most of the top ten mortgage banks that failed. California has 12 percent of the U.S. population, but between 2005 and 2007 more than 56 percent of America's subprime mortgages originated in California. It's estimated that in 2006, 9 percent of U.S. disposable income came from equity that people extracted from their houses: in California that figure was close to 20 percent. But most important for people who had to shelter themselves somewhere in the state, California was the epicenter of the housing price bubble.

In two decades California's median home price had gone up to more than double the national home price. Then, in just two years, it dropped by almost 40 percent. On a graph, that would look like the first nauseating hill on Coney Island's Cyclone roller coaster.

The bubble's burst left more than a third of California mortgages underwater. The national figure was 25 percent. But because house prices had been so high and mortgage terms so lenient, Californians were also much deeper underwater. (California housing statistics come from *California, Pivot of the Great Recession* by Ashok Bardhan of the Haas School of Business and Richard Walker of the University of California, Berkeley.)

These statistics meant that about a third of the people driving past me on California freeways were living in houses they couldn't afford to pay for yet couldn't sell. But when I talked to individuals living with this contradiction, I was struck, at first, by an insouciant or perhaps fey spirit. Two decades of life in the bubble had led to a different way of thinking about home and debt from what I was used to.

To my parents, a house was a good investment because (as they and their friends repeated like a mantra) "real estate always keeps pace with inflation." That didn't mean they were going to make a killing. It meant that house prices would rise enough over the years so that if, God forbid, they had to move out of Brooklyn, they could sell this house and buy a similar one somewhere else.

When they were ready to retire, my parents sold the house where they raised us, bought a smaller place for less money, deposited the difference in the bank, and congratulated themselves on their prudence. During all the years that they were paying off their mortgage, I never once heard my folks talk about how much our house was currently worth.

But California house prices rose so quickly during the bubble decades and were followed so avidly in the local media that few buyers could help thinking about the resale value of their homes.

If you buy a house to live in, you're a homeowner. If you buy a house to hold and then sell when the price goes up, that's called speculation. It's possible to be doing a bit of each in one's heart. But during the boom years the balance in the Golden State tilted till many seemed to think of their house more as an investment than a home.

To some folks it was the kind of investment you eventually cash in for one lump sum. Often they already counted that future appreciation as a solid part of their retirement savings.

Others thought of their homes as more like an interest- or dividend-paying investment whose returns they could use for current expenses. The U.S. Federal Reserve estimates that in 2005, Americans extracted $750 billion of equity from their houses through refinancing and spent two-thirds of that on personal consumption, home improvements, and credit card debt.

Still others seemed to believe they could have their appreciation and spend it too. You could periodically empty the house of equity and still retire on it when you finally sold it.

If this was true of the house you lived in, what about the house next door? During the housing boom it wasn't uncommon to buy condos two at a time. Turning over or "flipping" houses became something to brag about: speculation became an acceptable middle-class avocation.

When house prices suddenly dropped, many small speculators lost both their fantasy fortunes and every single penny of real cash that they'd put into their homes.

The first failed speculator I met was a charming mortgage saleswoman who displayed an edge-of-the-continent optimism about second chances that made it hard at first to think of her as a victim, even though she's now living in a trailer.

Meet a Mortgage Hustler

A professor told me about a bright UCLA student named Zita San Antonio who'd been evicted during finals week from a house she'd been renting from her mother.

I met the thirty-year-old for coffee and asked her to tell me about her eviction.

"Which one?" she answered.

"The eviction from your mother's house."

"Which one of those?" She played it deadpan. "This isn't the first recession where I got foreclosed out of the family home."

Zita (short for Zeneida) explained that her parents had emigrated from the Philippines in the 1970s. By the recession of the early 1990s they were well enough established in California to lose two university jobs—her father as a staff architect and her mother as a bookkeeper—both on the same University of California campus. As a result the San Antonios lost the home they lived in and a smaller property they rented out. At the time Zita, their first child born in America, was seventeen and ready for college.

"My early childhood was as secure and stable as can be," Zita assured me. "Both my parents had good jobs with traditional benefits. They got me into a gifted children's school; my expected trajectory was four-year college.

"But we lost the house, and the state of California enacted the first big educational cuts in my lifetime." (That recession was so deep that between 1991 and 1993, California lost 500,000 jobs. Its recession-related budget problems lingered until 1996.) "So I went to work and took some community college courses."

Fast-forward a decade to 2003.

Zita's parents are now living in Las Vegas. Her mother is involved in what Zita calls "multilevel businesses."

"In the Filipino community, I guess in all tight ethnic communities, there are these businesses where you make money if you bring more people in to sell. Yes, like Amway. But at Mom's level it was more like financial products, maybe insurance.

"In 2003, I hear from my mother that she's studying for a real estate broker's license to take advantage of the housing boom. When she started making real money selling mortgage loans in Las Vegas, it revived her dreams of flipping houses in California."

Meanwhile, a decade had passed for Zita too.

"I was working in an Internet company, a cool little start-up, but then it got taken over by a big L.A. real estate magnate." Unlike those of many of her colleagues, Zita's job wasn't outsourced to India; still, "working for a corporation like that will drive you either to substance abuse or socialism."

So Zita was ready when her mother approached her with an offer.

"She said, 'I'm making money now: I want to help you finish school.' So she and I basically agreed to go in on a house in Burbank. She'd put up the down payment, and I'd pay whatever I could afford in rent to supplement the mortgage payments. Her idea was that I'd get cheap rent and soon the skyrocketing house prices would produce equity that she could take out of the house and use to pay for my education.

"I moved in in 2004 and worked part-time for a couple of years while I went back to community college toward transferring to the university. In fall 2007, I transferred to UCLA, and that's when the real estate market plunged.

"And see, here's the thing with my mother, she has that business spirit of reckless optimism. She'd talk a little about her real estate but never let us know how much in trouble she was. But I should have guessed.

"She was always asking us to send her recruits, people she might be able to sell these loans to. I had never actually seen my mom pitch until I took her to some friends who were interested in buying a house. That's when I realized that her big market was subprime loans. So I started to send her copies of the show." One of Zita's part-time jobs was as technical producer for *Beneath the Surface*, an L.A. radio show that, at the height of the boom, featured guests who discussed the real estate crash to come. "I'm sending her articles like, 'This Can't Last,' 'You Have to Get Out.' And she's like, 'Yes, you're right, but we'll hold on one more year because the prices are still going up.'

"I felt like Cassandra: I'm looking right at the iceberg"—Greek mythology isn't Zita's specialty—"but no one will listen to me. I wasn't exactly listening to myself, either, because I thought I'd have time to move out at the end of the school year.

"So my mother's assuring me that everything is fine, and one day a few days before finals week for the winter quarter of 2008, I come home one day and I see a notice on my door. Everything on the premises must be removed in ten days. I took a picture of the sign. What I remember was like, 'This property is foreclosed and will be put up for auction on this date. You must vacate the premises by then.'

"So I'm," Zita says, giggling, "freaking out. Not only do I have to pack up a two-bedroom house in ten days and find a place to go, but it's happening during finals week. Wow, thanks, Mom, for telling me."

"So you and your mother didn't own the house together?" I try to get it straight. "I mean, you never got any of the earlier notices about falling behind on the payments?"

"No, we didn't own the house together, and no, I never got any notices, and I never got any financial help with school. But I did get cheap rent. A two-bedroom house for whatever I could pay. Sometimes that was as little as $400 a month. So absolutely, living in my mother's house was a leg up, a subsidy that allowed me to go to school full-time. I only had to earn living expenses. I guess the thing that made me angry with my mother is that she didn't say anything. She never told me she was in trouble. And then I get that notice—ten days!"

A federal regulation passed in 2009 grants paid-up tenants ninety days' notice to move out, but Zita didn't even think of consulting a lawyer. This college-educated anti-authoritarian complied immediately with an official-looking notice tacked on her door and moved out during finals week. With the help of a couple of extensions she got through the term with her usual high grades.

"And your parents," I asked, "how did they make it through their second American recession? Emotionally, I mean—two educated people who moved from Southeast Asia to California for economic opportunity, but they wind up living in a trailer in Las Vegas?"

"The first recession had the worse effect on my father," Zita says. "He was used to being able to provide for the family. But after a couple of unsuccessful business efforts, he took early retirement. I'm the youngest, so I had to go off on my own during a time when he had lost his job and his house. It wasn't how he expected to send me out into life."

She thinks a bit more about her parents. "My father has the peasant mentality—focused on security, though he supports my mother in everything she does. But my mother is the real Horatio

Alger type. Right now she's talking about getting into short sales. That means helping people get out of the houses you loaned them the money to get into."

"Short sale" was, for a time, the catchphrase and great hope for cleaning up the mortgage mess. But negotiations with banks usually got so complicated that the potential buyer often vanished before the sale came off. It takes a skilled and patient real estate broker to consummate a short sale.

"I guess you could say my mom is looking for ways to make up her own losses by cleaning off the bones of other people's wrecks."

"She sounds amazingly flexible," I said.

"She really is. And I love her to death. She's my mom. But she's like a lot of people who buy into the spirit of capitalism but don't have the capital. She's always looking for the big chance. But she's not from the class that will hear about the next pyramid scheme toward the beginning. She'll never be 'inside' enough to get out in time."

"But she's still geared up for the next big thing?" I asked.

"Oh yeah," Zita answered. "My mom is . . ." Her pause implied unstoppable. "You'll just have to meet her."

It's a quick trip from Las Vegas to Burbank: the San Antonios visit their daughters there often. Zita arranged for me to meet her parents at her married sister Korina's house. She, Zita, would join us after her last class.

Bibi San Antonio is a small, erect woman who gives herself an extra inch of height with a perky hairdo like that of her heroine,

Corazon Aquino. But Bibi doesn't need that inch to make a big impression.

I don't know of any orthography that will catch the way she can pipe three musical tones into a single syllable to express derision, surprise, and most of all amusement. I'll try using italics, but remember that while Zita's mother could be adamant, she was never loud or shrill.

"You write shorthand," Mrs. San Antonio said approvingly as we got started.

"But I can never read it back."

She laughed and told me how she'd won a full scholarship to the Philippine government's prestigious commercial high school. "At that time most business was in the hands of foreigners. The president wanted to train Filipinos to run companies. That's how I learned accounting, salesmanship, public relations. That president was assassinated.

"What is it that you want?" Mrs. San Antonio asked in her straightforward way.

"I want to tell people how it felt to be selling houses in California in those days when everyone thought things would just keep going up."

"Everyone but Zita," her mother reminded me. "She kept warning me. But I didn't think it was going to happen so *soon*." She takes a brief pause for regret. "Anyway, I was not selling houses. I was selling loans. Mortgage loans. And the houses were in Nevada. In 2003 to 2005, that's when I made a lot of money.

"I started as a loan officer in Las Vegas, but most of my clients were in California. I have friends from San Diego to San Francisco. I don't do cold calls, and I don't mail letters. What happens with me is once I work with a client, they're happy and I get referrals. That's because I empathize and I analyze their situation."

Bibi explained that there were "a myriad" of loan options and it was sometimes necessary to insist that her boss make the lender (the bank at the other end of the phone) offer a specific loan to a particular client. "It's not just a matter of 'You want a loan, I give you a loan.' No. Because if I give you the wrong loan, you suffer."

"Okay," I say, hoping she'll get specific. "Let's say I've seen a house that I want to live in."

"That's just one type loan, the buy-a-house-to-live-in. There are myriads of programs for that but . . ."

Buying a house to live in wasn't her interest, I could see, so I tried another scenario. "Let's say in 2001 I have a house in Richmond, California, that's worth $300,000 and I want to give each of my two children down payments to buy houses in the neighborhood."

"But what is your *plan*?" Bibi asks me. "Who is going to pay the loan back? Maybe I shouldn't give you the loan."

"Did you often turn people down?"

"Yes, many times. Because to make money, you have to hold this house for five years. Are you sure, just in case you lose your income, you can keep to a five-year plan?"

"Okay," I ask. "What is a good plan? What should I ask you for?"

"The best example: a lot of people owned homes in California, and the homes are valued very high. Let's say you own a house here. Your house is now valued at 1 million. Or let's say $500,000. All you need is to get $100,000 cash money to make a down payment on another house. You'll rent that out and hold it for two or five years, then sell it and make money.

"In other words"—Bibi's eyes are coming alive—"if you had a

home that you lived in for several years and you only have $100,000 mortgage left on it, suddenly it's worth $500,000. What are you going to do with that $400,000?

"Ah"—her voice mellows as she answers her own question—"let us buy houses in Las Vegas and then let them appreciate for three or five years and then sell. That was the big thing, the *big* thing. There were other purposes for loans, but that was mostly what my people were thinking.

"Refinance your home in California and then buy a house in Las Vegas. So now you have your house with a $300,000 mortgage and you own *two* houses, right?"

"Right," I say, suddenly realizing that this is classic speculation. "Did you sell mostly in the Filipino community?"

"Yes, a lot of medical people, doctors, nurses."

"Did you bring people together like at Tupperware parties?" I ask.

"*No.*" Bibi is almost offended. "No, it was always individually, always around a dining room table like this. Every situation is different, personal. If you're nearing retirement, can you afford to hold a mortgage for twenty years? If you're young, is your income steady? Nurses, will they remain here, or will they go back?

"The point was to put all the money you can into mortgages instead of putting your hard-earned money into the savings account. What were you getting, 1.7 percent? The appreciation thing is far better than the bank.

"But each person's life situation is different. You'd be surprised. That's why I got a lot of referrals because I really do diligent work. But how did it fall out?" I was amazed when Bibi brought that question up herself. "How did it all fall out?"

"That's what everyone's asking," I said.

"Please don't blame *people* in your book," Bibi appeals to me. "Don't blame people for buying houses they couldn't afford. Well, maybe there are those. But if you really examine the matter, people bought the houses in Las Vegas because there was a *plan*, a plan to take care of themselves. Now, how did the plan fall apart?"

I shrug, eager to hear her explanation.

"Remember," Bibi says, "it was a five-year plan. But none of us knew what Wall Street was doing. We thought it was going to be the way it *was*. The way it was all those years. You know, your house appreciates and then . . .

"Remember, those loans were given by mortgage companies like, let's say, Bank of America or Wells Fargo. But those banks got money from Goldman Sachs, and Goldman Sachs got money by betting against the houses. I told you there were myriads of loan programs. By the end they were concocting loans just to sell to investors, loans that they knew would make the clients fail. Then companies like AIG, they took our loans and . . ."

Bibi San Antonio is a keen observer of the world in front of her eyes, but Goldman Sachs and AIG conduct their business above her eye level. She seemed to realize that she didn't know exactly what the Wall Street banks did with the mortgages she wrote, or how exactly they caused the crash. So she returned to the world she knew.

"We were working on the appreciation of the value and suddenly . . . If the value had just stopped growing, we would have been okay. But it *fell*, so everybody is upside down. But nobody knew it was coming."

"Except Zita," I reminded her.

"Yes, yes, my daughter. She is a genius. She is the only person that told me, 'Mom, don't do that, because it's going to fall apart.' I said, 'Well, maybe it will fall apart, but after five years.'

"I was working in a five-year plan myself, because I was making a lot of money, and money was accumulated in our house. And you can't just put your hard-earned money into the bank. So we bought houses too."

"That shows you were an honest salesperson," I said.

"Yes, we had the same plan that we sold to others. Would you believe that a house I bought for 260,000 is sold for 90,000?

"One house that I lived in for a while in Las Vegas, I was able to sell it on a short sale. Two other houses, they were going to be short sales, but they were foreclosed because . . ." She begins to mumble, and I catch "mortgage company," "try to negotiate," "lower the balance." Bibi then decides to forget the frustrating details and just give the final score.

"*Any*way, it's short sale one, foreclose two, but not the house in Burbank. That's the one I was able to save."

"Burbank?!"

"It's only nine hundred square feet, $390,000. I only bought one in California because it's expensive. But one good thing about me, when I bought a house, I always put down 20 percent, so in the end . . ."

Zita's mother saved the Burbank house?! Wait a minute. This started when I met a student who had to move during finals week because the house she was renting from her mother was foreclosed. But her mother says she still owns it. As I was about to delve into the Burbank mystery, Korina's husband, John, arrived home from work with sausages to grill. Zita came through the door shortly after.

"Your mother called you a genius," I said in greeting her. "I bet she never says it to your face."

"Yes she does." Mother and daughter hugged, and Zita went scavenging in the refrigerator for ready food. At no signal that I heard, Mr. San Antonio emerged from the den, and the family gathered around the table. The soup was lovely. Korina grows vegetables in the yard. She was trying to show her parents that food can taste good without a lot of salt. Bibi had had two strokes, I was surprised to hear.

"They eat what I send home with them," Korina said. "But in Las Vegas there's all the $3.99 buffets. And of course it's a sin to waste food," she chided her parents. "So if you take it, you have to eat it all."

As the table was being cleared, I found myself alone with Bibi again and asked immediately about the Burbank foreclosure.

"That was Indy Bank—I'm sorry, sometimes my memory—I mean Indy*Mac*." (Bibi makes fewer word slips than most people I interview. Imagine her before the strokes.)

"When your payment is up-to-date, when you don't have a delinquency, they will not negotiate a mortgage modification. If you stop your payment, then after three months, or six months, depends, they will start negotiating."

So Bibi stopped payments to get negotiations going.

"I wanted them to lower the principal; they only asked, 'How much can you pay?'"

"But wait," I said, "Zita got an eviction notice."

"I was negotiating with them, and it's part of the process that they will give you the default notice. Maybe sometimes a possibly improper foreclosure is done too." Bibi uttered this last bit about improper foreclosures as a throwaway line and went on describing her useless negotiations with IndyMac in some detail. Then finally she said: "We were not getting anywhere, and I was ready to let it go. But right then IndyMac went bankrupt, and the FDIC [Federal Deposit Insurance Corporation] took over. The FDIC was *good*, *very* good, because of that lady . . . Yes, Sheila Bair."

Sheila Bair, a Republican who first came to Washington as legal counsel on Kansas senator Bob Dole's staff, was appointed head of the FDIC in 2006 by George Bush. As early as 2001, Bair warned about a possible wave of defaults when adjustable rate mortgages reset. She tried unsuccessfully to get the most dangerous and abusive mortgage terms modified even before the crash.

In the run-up to the financial crisis, IndyMac and several other banks went bankrupt and were taken over by the FDIC in accordance with normal, well-established practices for resolving the affairs of insolvent banks.

Bibi described how the FDIC, under Bair's leadership, temporarily stopped the adverse procedures and sent professionals to assess her financial situation and negotiate a deal. They didn't grant the principal reduction she wanted, but they set a monthly payment she could meet by renting the house. "Twelve hundred dollars they wanted—it comes to $1,500 with insurance and property tax."

"Wait, the Burbank house is now rented? You own it and rent it out?"

Bibi told me with some pride how, rejecting agents, she herself located a tenant eager to use the good local schools. "I asked $1,900; my expenses are $1,500; I let her bargain it down to $1,800. They're good tenants. All I ask her is to take care of the yard. I used to pay this young man $65 just to take care of the small front yard."

Didn't Mrs. San Antonio understand what her genius daughter went through when she was foreclosed during finals week? Didn't Zita ever ask her mother if she really had to move out in ten days?

"So I make a family happy, and the payments are covered. I told my kids I'll hold on to the Burbank house till whatever my husband and I decide. But right now it's cleaner to live in Las Vegas."

What kind of *Rashomon* story is this? Zita races to empty a two-bedroom house and find a new place during finals week of her first year at the university. But in her mother's account the "possibly improper" foreclosure notice is only a footnote. I wanted to get this mother and daughter together. But before Zita returned, Mrs. San Antonio excused herself to join the men. "My Lakers are playing."

But I asked about the Burbank house when I got the two sisters alone.

"As soon as the FDIC took over, they stopped all foreclosures." That's Korina's first recollection.

"You're sure you really had to move?" I ask Zita.

"Yes. Remember that last day we ripped out all the fixtures?"

Her sister doesn't contradict that detail. It's just that her focus was on their mother's struggle to bargain with the bank.

"She was still in the midst of negotiating," Korina says, recalling her mother's frustrations. "She talked to some rep who didn't even know that a foreclosure notice had been sent."

"She didn't know until I called her," Zita says, confirming that part.

"But as soon as the FDIC took over, they called her right back," Korina recalls.

"I didn't know it was the FDIC thing that turned it around,"

Zita says. "I just remember four or six months later putting the fixtures back in."

The pieces almost fit together now. Everyone was surprised on the day that a foreclosure notice landed on the door, and everyone participated in ripping out fixtures and putting them back months later. It's just that some people were focused on saving the house, while some, or at least one, were focused on saving the term's work. Zita moved out shortly before her mother's deus ex machina, Sheila Bair, descended to take charge.

Sheila Bair is widely credited with preventing pre-crash bank runs by operating insolvent banks with a minimum of disruption as she applied standard resolution procedures to balance the interests of depositors, borrowers, and investors.

But before the crash the FDIC's authority to "resolve" failing banks didn't extend to bank holding companies like Citi or to various uninsured, unregulated, nonbank financial institutions that were in trouble. The post-crash Dodd-Frank financial reform bill is supposed to give the FDIC wider authority the next time.

Even before those reforms, however, many of the FDIC's time-tested procedures could have been applied to the rescued institutions. Those standard resolution procedures usually begin with taking control away, at least temporarily, from the existing management. Resolutions also usually involve some losses to bank bondholders.

But both the Bush and the Obama administrations abandoned the traditional resolution approach in favor of simply handing $700 billion to the existing managements of financial institutions deemed too big to fail. I wonder what today's political and economic environment would be like if our government had conducted its rescue in the spirit of a resolution rather than a bailout.

Save Your Cash, Not Your Credit

Before I left Burbank, Bibi San Antonio wanted me to understand that when the crisis hit, she'd acted honorably. As soon as she grasped that house prices weren't coming back up, she contacted her old clients and advised them to stop paying on the mortgages she'd arranged for them.

"I have told many people, 'You'd be a fool to keep paying the $200,000 on a house worth $70,000. If you want to live, walk away. Walk away from it!' "

She'd done that herself in Nevada and had been prepared to walk away from the Burbank house if she couldn't get a deal to her liking.

"And you're really not worried about past foreclosures if you have to apply for a new mortgage someday?" I asked Bibi.

"*No.*" Her tone says, "Are you some kind of child?" "You know what happened: you explain what happened. You're applying for something *now*, and you have the right income *now*. I can't be held captive for something like that!"

"Do you sell your children in order to make the monthly payments?!" Korina interjected. She and her husband had also walked away from a couple of properties after the crash.

"But most people worry about their credit," I objected.

"You only need credit in order to borrow money," Bibi explained. "It's better to *have* money. That's why I tell all my old clients, '*Save your cash, not your credit.*' "

A year after I met the San Antonios in Burbank, Zita came to New York for an academic conference. She was a graduate student by then. I asked whether her mom and dad were still living in their trailer.

"That's a funny story," she said, and explained that her parents had come into a chunk of money related to a Las Vegas hotel investment they'd pulled out of before the place was built.

"I don't know the exact details," Zita said, "but when the dust from the lawsuits settled, they received a check for $175,000. So I said"—here Zita becomes the mature adult—" 'Mom, why don't you buy a house in California?—a house to *live in*?'

"She looked at me and said, 'I can buy *two* houses in Las Vegas.'

"I said, 'Mom, please, I don't want you to die in the desert.' "

In the end the San Antonios bought neither two houses to invest in nor one house to live in. Residential property was still too risky, Bibi judged; no one knew when it would hit bottom. So she put the money into California commercial real estate in the form of a medical building her son-in-law got them into. Zita reported, "It pays them back monthly, like an annuity, Mom told me—about $2,000 a month."

So the San Antonios still live in a Las Vegas trailer park—"That $6,000 trailer Dad bought 'just in case' is the best investment they ever made," says their daughter—and they supplement their Social Security and Mr. San Antonio's pension with returns from a commercial property. If that goes bad, Bibi San Antonio will surely be ready to move, probably just a little bit late, into the next big thing.

Chapter Eight

STRATEGIC DEFAULT

First-Class Scofflaws

All over California, solid citizens were discussing whether to stop paying their bills. At the time of my visit about 35 percent of California mortgages were "underwater." Eleven percent of mortgages were seriously delinquent, and many more homeowners were about to stop paying. Since unemployment was also high there—it was 12.4 percent when the national figure was a little over 9 percent— many would soon have little choice. But a shocking number of people with jobs and savings were making calculated decisions about welshing on their debts. In the lending industry that's called strategic default.

Bibi San Antonio is an ardent and unusually open champion of that strategy. But you don't need a formal interview to get in on California's default debate. Just say the word "mortgage" in a public place, and it turns into a housing seminar.

On my way back from Burbank, I mentioned the housing crash in the airport waiting area, and a man volunteered that he and his wife had talked it over with their financial planner, and, he said, "We decided to cut our losses."

"What about your credit?" asked a well-coiffed woman who was traveling with her grown daughter.

The man explained that he and his wife didn't rely on credit for anything but buying a house. They planned to rent, at least until house prices stabilized. He figured that in a few years lenders would look back at this period and say, "Oh, you got caught up in the bubble, never mind."

But what the well-coiffed woman really wanted to know was, if she walked away from her current house, would her credit be good enough—right now—to buy the vacant house down the block?

"She always did like that corner house," the daughter said, trying to turn it into a joke. "If you buy it," she teased her mother, "you can finally take down that clothesline that was gonna lower our property value."

But the woman was obviously serious and moved to the seat next to me to talk it over.

She liked the neighborhood; the corner house was $300,000 cheaper than it had been a few years earlier; it was the house she should have bought in the first place; and now it was even painted to her taste—blue with lavender trim. (The neighbor had taken her advice about repainting before moving out so suddenly.)

The challenge would be to find a mortgage broker with whom she could lay her cards on the table. She needed to find out, *in advance*, whether she could qualify for a decent mortgage on the corner house if she stopped paying on her old house in the middle of the block. In a way she was trying to accomplish the same thing as government modification programs. They aimed to settle people in houses that were closer to today's market prices without making them actually move. The lavender-loving woman's plan was to move a few doors down to a post-boom-priced house.

Bibi San Antonio was the only Southern California mortgage broker I knew. But a couple of the others who joined our conversation were able to give her some names in her area. All these would-be defaulters and abettors appeared to me to be upper-middle-class travelers. At least one was flying business class. Clearly, sneaking away from a mortgaged house was no longer something only a shameless scofflaw would contemplate.

Co-conspirators

Cindi and Amanda are friends and colleagues whose work involves giving consultations and seminars throughout Northern California. They made time to meet me at Amanda's Benicia condo at the end of a long business day. Both women were experts at "accessing data," as Cindi put it, and had just started using that expertise to decide whether to keep paying their respective mortgages.

"I had already made some money flipping a condo," Cindi explained. To me the word "flipping" had an illicit connotation that it clearly didn't have to the two friends. In prerecession California, real estate speculation had been an acceptable middle-class activity.

In 2006, Cindi put her whole flipping profit—$100,000—into a down payment on a small $475,000 house near the water in Solano County. She loved the place and fondly described her new marble countertops. But the house would now sell for no more than $200,000. "Yes, I'm down over 60 percent," Cindi confirmed for me. But her minimum mortgage payment was still $2,300 a month.

Amanda and her husband live out of state, and commuting to her job was getting difficult. In 2006, a California pied-à-terre seemed like a good investment, and Cindi helped Amanda house hunt. At $390,000 this small two-bedroom condo in a well-landscaped development way north of the Bay Area seemed like the best buy they could find. But only three years later, Amanda estimated that she couldn't get more than $200,000 for it. (Her estimate proved to be $100,000 high.)

Cindi apologized for urging her friend to make the purchase, but Amanda pooh-poohed her guilt. "Back then, we *all* thought prices would just keep going up. Don't you remember?"

Just a couple of weeks before I met them, Amanda had returned from a trip home to find that the neighbor on the other side of her wall had disappeared, one family below had stopped paying their mortgage, and another one said he would have to stop paying as soon as his low teaser rate expired. To top it off, she saw that she could rent one of the luxury units in the development—"the same layout as this but with dark wood floors"—for $1,100 a month while she was paying $2,300 a month to "own" and building no equity with that payment.

Amanda could afford to keep making the mortgage payments, she said, but "it makes you feel sick to throw a couple of thousand dollars out the window every month." But Cindi, who was divorced and living on only one income, would eventually be caught in an "affordability bind," she said. Her plan had been to stay in the house until she retired, then take the profit and move someplace cheaper. But that hope was gone for good, she recognized, and "I won't be able to keep making the payments when I retire."

"Basically, we have three choices," Amanda said. "We can hold the property and keep paying more than it will ever be worth again. We can try to negotiate something with our bank around a short sale or a loan modification. Or the third choice is we can let it go to foreclosure, ruin our credit, and walk away."

It was time to get serious, so they divided up the research.

Cindi was checking into government programs. Neither of them was eligible for the Home Affordable Modification Program, or HAMP, she'd discovered. Their houses were too far underwater. But Washington was about to announce new guidelines. She was pretty sure they'd both be above the income limits, but she'd keep on top of it.

Meanwhile, Amanda was trying to answer the question that bedeviled so many distressed homeowners: Do you help or hurt yourself with the bank if you stop paying? A realtor told her to stop; it was only then that the bank would deal with you. She tried to check that out at a title company.

"They said, 'No ethical realtor would ever tell somebody that.' But they didn't deny it."

Amanda tried to hire the title company to negotiate for her, but it wouldn't take her money. The representative told her truthfully that her mortgage company, Bank of America, would not negotiate with a third party.

The blue-and-lavender lady who coveted the corner house didn't think of herself as a criminal. Still, she was hesitant to ask her default questions directly. Not these two. "If you want to make the best decision, you need all the information you can get," Cindi said.

The two friends apologized for having no definitive answers yet, but they'd just started their research, and as they explained, these had been busy weeks of very long workdays. It seemed like the cue for me to leave.

I was still mildly shocked to hear well-dressed professionals coolly consider default. But I was beginning to realize that white Californians who drive new cars and speak TV announcer English may be poorer than they look. I don't know exactly what these women earn; it's enough to make air commuting worthwhile. But apparently, it hadn't been enough to own middle-class homes in pre-crash California. At least not as I understand home ownership.

Amanda bought her condo with a $10,000 original payment. Cindi's mortgage had an interest-only option. Since she usually made that minimum, all-interest payment, she wasn't building equity.

In effect, they were renting from the bank with an option to share in the appreciation when their houses were sold. But that option was now worthless. Their houses had been so overpriced that they won't return to their prerecession values within these women's lifetimes. These are hard facts, but the two friends were ready to face them squarely and try to come out of it as well as they could.

Two years later Cindi was still living in her Solano County home. There'd been a shake-up on the job in the meantime, and she'd accepted early retirement. She'd predicted that she wouldn't be able to make her minimum mortgage payment once she retired. But with interest rates so low, the interest-only option had gone down by $1,200 a month. Since she could afford the payment, since she genuinely liked the house, and since she had to live somewhere, she stayed put for the meantime.

Amanda had also been affected by the job shake-up. She now works out of Southern California. Shortly after my visit she'd opted for a short sale. She quickly found a customer ready to buy her Benicia condo for the then going price of $100,000. But when she contacted Bank of America, she was told by a clerk that the bank couldn't start any sorts of negotiations because the mortgage payments were up-to-date. Amanda reluctantly stopped paying. After ten months of refusals and reversals the bank finally approved the short sale, and Amanda moved out with no debt.

"The bank could have had the same $100,000 without first giving me ten months of free rent," Amanda said. "Fortunately, the buyer stuck with me."

In the course of her research Amanda heard that her bank was even slower about foreclosures than short sales. She realized that she could probably have lived rent-free in her condo for longer if she dropped the short sale and simply waited for a foreclosure. But she and her husband wanted to do as little damage to their credit rating as possible.

This is how Amanda summed up her experience as a California homeowner: "It cost us about fifty points on our credit rating. That's less than I thought it would. It also cost us all of $10,000 that we originally put in. And for five years we paid $2,000 a month in mortgage and owners' fees for a place we could have rented for half that. I would call it an expensive rental."

Chapter Nine

AN UPRIGHT MAN

Carrots for Bankers

When housing prices plummeted and people started defaulting, the first reaction after shock was blame. Irresponsible banks had victimized borrowers. No, irresponsible borrowers had victimized banks. (This is still a provocative topic, and we'll get back to it.)

But some people said it takes two to make a loan, so forget the blame and let borrowers and lenders share the loss, as would commonly happen with commercial or industrial real estate debt. The traditional way to do that is through a mortgage modification that lowers the principal to something between the new market value and the old mortgage debt. With a modification, lenders accept a loss, or a "haircut," as they say in the debt business. In many cases the banks may ultimately collect more that way than they would through foreclosure, while homeowners get to stay in their homes.

The argument for modifications wasn't purely humanitarian, however. The housing collapse triggered immediate massive unemployment. California alone lost some 600,000 jobs in the construction, building supplies, real estate, and related financial sectors.

But new home building couldn't pick up while millions of foreclosed houses were still coming onto the market. Keeping people in their homes was widely prescribed as a job, not just a housing relief measure.

So the brand-new Obama administration immediately proposed the Helping Families Save Their Homes Act, one feature of which gave bankruptcy judges the right to lower a homeowner's mortgage debt as part of a bankruptcy settlement. Bankruptcy judges already have the power to modify mortgages or "smack down" the debt on vacation homes, farms, and yachts. The Obama proposal would have given homeowners the same leverage that those yacht, farm, and vacation home owners have in negotiating mortgage modifications before a bankruptcy judge can impose a smackdown.

The new president seemed stunned at how easily the banks, then at the height of their disgrace, were able to smack down the smackdown provision. Their lobbying of both parties was overt, venal, illogical, and completely effective. The quick defeat of this widely agreed-upon recovery measure set the pattern. The Obama administration went on, as it would so often, to propose an insufficient, ineffective compromise.

That's how we got the Home Affordable Modification Program, or HAMP, a mortgage modification plan that was all carrots, no sticks. Banks would receive bonuses for each successful modification they made. Banks that signed up for HAMP had the obligation to accept and process applications, but whether they then granted a modification was strictly up to them.

Within a couple of years the administration acknowledged that the results of the voluntary program had been "disappointing." They had prepared to subsidize between 3 and 4 million mortgage modifications, but in two years the banks approved only some 670,000.

When I arrived in California, the disappointing results were already trickling in anecdotally. People dealing with different major lenders complained in almost the same words that the paperwork was overwhelming, that they were asked for the same information over and over, and that the process seemed to have no end. While many were applying, few were chosen. No one I questioned had heard of anyone who'd actually had his mortgage modified.

But if anyone was capable of dealing with paperwork, it was Balty Alatas.

Before he was laid off, Mr. Alatas earned $80,000 a year at a private company that trained professionals working in the area of child welfare. Most of his firm's clients had been state or municipal agencies. As a top administrator, Balty not only had to work his way through government paperwork in order to get the contracts; he'd also helped create curricula to teach field workers how to handle the paperwork necessary to access services for needy children. But when their government clients suffered big budget cuts, his employer had to cut its staff in turn. Mr. Alatas was one of the last to go.

When I phoned him at home in Vallejo, he'd been out of work for a year and had been negotiating a mortgage modification with Bank of America for nine months.

Balty and I speculated about the bank's motives for making the modification process so complicated. He was coming to believe that the baroquely embellished procedures were deliberately designed to give people just enough hope to keep them paying on the mortgage as long as humanly possible. That's what he himself seemed to be doing.

I tended to think that the banks were confused, overwhelmed, and making it up as they went along. Neither of us was sure of our analysis. Balty suggested I come examine his files to see what I made of them.

Sticks for Borrowers

Vallejo is twenty-five miles north of San Francisco. According to my map, we were already in his neighborhood. But there wasn't any neighborhood. The city once housed the largest shipyard on the West Coast. It was finally closed in 1996, and nothing had replaced it. The only open enterprise I'd seen since I'd entered Vallejo was a gas station. The only person I'd encountered on the street was a thin pregnant woman who talked to herself loudly enough for us to hear her through closed car windows.

Finally, according to the map, we were just about at the Alatas house. But I couldn't find any street signs or even anything that looked like a street. Then I tilted my head, just slightly, and saw a tiny landscaped cul-de-sac shimmering like the mirage of a 1950s suburb. The fantasy came complete with polished house numbers, so it was easy to find the address.

Mr. Alatas settled me under the backyard arbor and brought out a tea tray. "Are those real?!" I pointed at what seemed a second mirage. My host picked a glowing fruit from a bush, and I shaved the zest of a Meyer lemon into my cup. What an aroma.

Now properly refreshed, I took note of the fifty-five-year-old man, his mildly frazzled and younger wife, and their appropriately playful four-year-old son, Stefan. The name Balty had conjured up a jolly, and probably plump, elf. But this Balty, short for Balthazar, seemed a temperate and sober man whose solid frame suggested dependability.

First I asked about this Edenic enclave.

"It has twenty-six homes," Balty told me. "In the last two, two and a half years, about eight, so almost a third, of the owners have been distressed. We've had neighbors who moved out in the middle of the night, and on the east side of the circle you'll notice three houses in a row whose yards look like they haven't been taken care of in a while."

I asked how he and his wife wound up there. He answered by telling me how his Indonesian family wound up in Holland. His father had been in the Dutch air force. Indeed his family had served loyally in the Dutch colonial military for generations. "When Indonesia gained independence in the late 1940s, my dad and three thousand other men had the option of going to prison or leaving the country. So they went to Holland, where they were spread out in military camps."

"How did your family get from Holland to Vallejo?"

Balty's grandmother bought the house in the 1980s as a base for several young relatives going to school in the Napa area. After the last of them returned to Indonesia, the house stood vacant. But Balty's part of the family settled in California, and in 1996 he moved in and began paying $600 a month to cover the mortgage. When he and Debbie married in 2001, they decided it was time to buy the house from his grandmother.

"It can be hard for people to blend households," I suggested. (It was a second marriage for Balty, and he seemed to be a person of deliberate habits.)

"Well, we've renovated just about everything since we bought it," Debbie said. "So it's become *ours* over the years."

The renovation was part of a five-year plan. Debbie, like Balty, had worked in child welfare. When they married, they'd decided to "give something back." Over their married years they'd been foster parents to five children, three who had been successfully reunited with their parents, one out of the house to whom they still acted as legal guardian, and Stefan, whom they'd adopted soon after he was born.

The plan began with expanding the small house to accommodate the children. (At one point Balty and Debbie were sleeping on mats on the floor.) But there was no way Stefan would go to Vallejo schools. They'd seen what some of the foster kids endured.

So the five-year plan, as Balty summarized it, was "refinance, redo, and, by the time Stefan enters kindergarten, sell the home. We didn't know that the market would fall out on us within two years."

Their mortgage debt, including the original purchase plus $150,000 borrowed for the renovation, was currently $390,000. "We had this house appraised once at $625,000," Balty said. "I'd be surprised if we could get $225,000 now."

The bust that deflated individual house values wrecked the city's already rocky finances, and Vallejo filed for bankruptcy. Firemen and policemen accepted 35 percent pay cuts. Two of three police stations were closed; the third is open to the public only three days a week. A city official advised citizens to use the 911 emergency number sparingly.

In many recession-hit cities, business shifts from better shops to the discount stores. In Vallejo, the Walmart moved out.

Even before the recession, Vallejo public schools had been unacceptable to the Alatases. Now the schools were worse, but they couldn't move away, so Debbie was preparing to homeschool her son in the fall. Mrs. Alatas had been a stay-at-home mom at the time that Balty lost his job. She'd now found a few freelance jobs as a parenting coach (a kind of super-nanny). I judged from the exercises on Stefan's little desk that she was probably qualified to teach him at home. But she didn't like the idea of keeping him isolated like that.

The economic crisis had boxed them into a tiny cul-de-sac, and they couldn't afford to move out. But how long could they keep paying enough to stay locked in?

After Balty lost his job, the couple continued paying their $2,900 mortgage for two months. "He had vacation pay and stuff," Debbie explained. "Then my parents began helping, thinking he would have a job by now."

Lest I take that as an implied criticism, Debbie made sure I understood that her husband job hunted tirelessly. "It got to the point where I actually asked him to only put in a few hours a day because Stefan and I were here in the home and we were losing him to the job search." In the last nine months her husband had had six interviews, she told me.

I gasped at that low number, then realized that it was a tribute for a middle-aged man to get to the interview stage on jobs for which there had been many applicants. "On three of those I was one of two finalists," Balty told me. "But if you're one of two and you're not chosen, all you can think of is, what more can I possibly do to actually get it?"

Turning to another source of despair, Balty cleared a space and set down a pile of printed correspondence about a foot and a half thick. He also kept a handwritten log of his phone communications with Bank of America. Each entry included the date, the name of the customer service representative he spoke to, anyone he'd been transferred to, and a brief summary of the conversation. Some of the entries were annotated with a smiley, frowny, or neutral face. That bit of whimsy surprised me.

The icons, Balty explained, described the tone of the conversation rather than anything about the outcome. "You can't tell much about the progress you're making by what one person said on the phone. But it feels better to talk to someone pleasant."

The first papers I drew randomly from the stack were requests for documents verifying income and expenses. Like everyone else who'd entered modification negotiations, Balty complained, "I kept getting letters asking for the same documents over and over." He'd learned that it was quicker to send things again than to try to locate the person at the bank who'd already received and even discussed the documents with him.

"No matter how many times they ask, I've always complied in full," Balty said.

"I bet you didn't submit this in full," I said, indicating a request for utility bills and death certificates.

"Well, there hadn't been any death in the family. That was my response." He had, however, resubmitted the utility bills.

One letter I pulled from the pile indicated that Balty's case was being transferred to another unit within the bank. To me that sounded hopeful, especially since he'd been transferred to the Hope Team. ("It had something to do with the stimulus package," Balty said.) More recently, he'd been transferred to the Escalation Q Unit. An escalation also sounded hopeful. But in Balty's experience each transfer meant that he had to start all over with someone new.

The letter on the top of the pile was in answer to a formal complaint he'd lodged. I read a paragraph:

> *At times the process can be repetitive and lengthy. Our*
> *work-out negotiators work diligently to minimize delays,*
> *however, at times unforeseen occurrences beyond anyone's*
> *control may further delay the process. We appreciate your*
> *continued patience as we work toward completing the mod-*
> *ification of your loan.*

The bank's own description of its "repetitive and lengthy" process with "unforeseen occurrences beyond anyone's control" sounded a lot like Balty's description.

After examining this and other documents, I still couldn't make up my mind whether Bank of America's modification process was carefully crafted to squeeze out the last possible payment—I could imagine a consultant saying, "Statistics indicate that people will continue to pay for an average of two and a half months if given a direct phone extension to call"—or if it was an ad hoc agglomeration of procedures that grew up while the bank tried to figure out what to do with all these underwater houses.

Whether the process was planned or ad hoc, the bank was stalling. To prevent homeowners from stalling in return, its first modification communication warned that any mortgage payments missed during the negotiations may be reported to credit bureaus and that the bank could go forward with foreclosure regardless of the state of the negotiations.

I could understand why the bank would want to delay making a decision while the borrower was still paying in full. But I was losing track of Balty's strategy. Mr. Alatas was fifty-five years old and unemployed. There seemed to be no way he could go on paying any mortgage, no matter how modified, unless he found a good job. But that was statistically unlikely. Mightn't it be better to stop paying his mortgage sooner and save some cash for the inevitable move?

As Balty continued pulling documents from the pile, I remembered a scene from *Catch-22*. Yossarian is tending a soldier's arm wound when he notices that the man's guts are spilling out. Since there's nothing he can do about the guts, he turns back and busies himself bandaging the arm. Was Balty's meticulous form filing a way to hold the truly insoluble at bay?

"What if you tried to sell now?" I asked the Alatases.

"I think we would owe about twice as much as we could get from a sale," Balty answered.

"Well, what if you just stopped paying?"

"That's what everybody says," Debbie said with a sigh. "But we've worked really hard to have good credit."

"And maintain that credit," Balty added. "And besides, it's . . ." He seemed almost embarrassed as he said the next word: "Ethics. It's a question of ethics or—"

"Feeling responsible," his wife said to help him out.

"My parents did not cross two continents and live on three continents in order to move backward. They were serious about what they wanted out of life for themselves and for their future generations, and that meant living up to traditional values and commitments."

To Balty's father, honor had required remaining loyal to the Dutch colonial army till the very last minute. His son seemed to be almost as loyal to Bank of America.

So they sat amid the lemon trees in a landscaped cul-de-sac out of which they daren't send their child to play. They were trapped sociologically, trapped ethically, and trapped financially.

As I was leaving, Debbie gave me some lemons, and Balty printed out a map to my next stop. I couldn't imagine the Alatases stealing away from their house in the middle of the night. But it was even harder to imagine them paying all that Bank of America demands on their underwater property. Something's gotta give. As the couple waved from the doorway, I worried that it would be Balty's heart.

Two Surprises

A year later I checked back with the Alatases and got two surprises.

First, Balty has a full-time, permanent executive job. He works at his former level for a company that does the same kind of training as his old firm. He'd taken a $15,000 pay cut, but, he said, "Everyone in my position is ready to make that kind of sacrifice. We're just happy to be working."

"How'd you find it?" I asked.

"I spotted it on Craigslist, I called, I came in, they hired me."

"You must have been a perfect fit," I said.

"I am a perfect fit," he answered factually. "But when I came on board, I kept looking over my shoulder, sure that I was going to get axed. My program is growing, my supervisor likes what I'm doing, but I'm still looking over my shoulder. It's PTSD [post-traumatic stress disorder]. I'm sure it's not that uncommon for folks who've gone through what we've gone through in the last few years. I wonder how long it lasts."

Follow-up studies from previous recessions indicate that after a decade most workers who'd been laid off hadn't reached their pre-layoff expected earning levels. But I've never seen a study of how long it takes to recover pre-layoff emotional levels. I have no idea how long Balty's PTSD is likely to last.

I wonder about the lasting emotional effects on children who've watched their parents live through long bouts of unemployment or other forms of insecurity.

"How's Stefan?" I asked. "Is Debbie homeschooling him?"

When their four-year-old hadn't made it through the lottery for Vallejo's one charter school, the Alatases enrolled him in a Catholic preschool. "We liked the program and he *loves* it. My other children were athletes, but school is going to be his thing!"

Even over the phone (Balty was talking to me on his commute from work), I could feel the warmth as he described his son singing his heart out in a preschool choral performance.

"But it's five hundred a month, and that is cheap for a private school. Five hundred a month for kindergarten?"

Schools open in September, but Balty hadn't started his new job until November. I wondered aloud how the couple had paid Stefan's fees in the interim. "Your in-laws again or . . . ?"

Here's where I got the second surprise.

After a year and a half of negotiations, Bank of America had formally rejected the Alatases' request for a mortgage modification.

"When Bank of America sent us that letter 'you've been denied,' we stopped paying."

"You stopped paying your mortgage?!"

"What I've told every single Bank of America person who's called since then is 'We worked with you in good faith for a year and a half. I understand that from your perspective me continuing paying you would look good. But if I pay for another year and a half, what will change?' Now we're using some of that money for school fees."

"So what do you think is gonna happen?"

"The bank basically says, 'Well, we haven't moved on your house.' And I say, 'If you want it, come take it. I was out of work for fifteen months; we depleted our savings; we paid you in full for a year and a half. You've taken practically everything else we have. If you want this house, come take it.' They haven't done that yet."

"You know, Balty, you sound terrific."

"We're still willing to work with them if they give us something. But right now we're not paying them anything, if that makes sense?"

"Not only does it make sense," I said, "it seems almost liberating."

"It truly is," Balty agreed. "Before we were kind of feeling like we were bad consumers, we weren't responsible people, all those things. But after having tried to work with the bank for a year and a half, I know that we were not irresponsible. *I know we're not deadbeats.*"

"Was that a dog?" I asked.

"Well, I just got home," Balty answered. "Did you want to check in with Debbie?"

When I heard Debbie's voice—sweet and still tired sounding—I sputtered about how often I'd put off calling them. "I feel like a ghoul calling people whose bad outcome is my story. But Balty's job, Stefan's school, you're my first happy ending."

"Yes, we're thrilled," she said.

"What will you do now?" I asked. "Do you want to stay in the house as long as you can, or are you just waiting for a chance to move on, or to . . . ?"

Debbie cut off the list of options. "I kind of resigned myself a while back to taking it one day at a time. If you try to plan, there's so many ifs that it gets overwhelming."

What a surprise! Balty Alatas stopped paying his mortgage and intends to live for free till either they kick him out or he finds it convenient to leave. I had been looking for a trickster ready to say, "Show me the mortgage." But here was a solid citizen saying, "Okay, you own this house. But so what?"

Chapter Ten

THE HOUSE BELONGS TO THEM

Her Day in Court

When I was in California in 2009, creditors seemed to be fore-closing slowly, or at least erratically. In 2011 a group of mortgage investors who used Bank of America as their servicer were awarded billions of dollars for losses suffered due to delayed foreclosures. Their lawsuit revealed that the bank had been taking an average of a year and a half from a default to foreclosure. Other mortgage servicers were having similar, though perhaps less extreme, dif-ficulties dealing with all the delinquencies. That's one reason why savvy borrowers like Cindi, Amanda, Balty, and Bibi San Antonio had the leeway to investigate their options and, on occasion, even time their ousters to suit their own convenience. But that wasn't the case for everyone.

There had been over half a million repossessions in California between 2007 and 2009. Many of them involved agonizing uncer-tainty, as I was reminded when I attended a court session in the predominantly black city of Richmond, California.

There were no microphones in the Contra Costa County courtroom, so I missed a lot of what was said. But at one point the defendant, a solid woman with a strong voice, asked, "When will this happen, Your Honor?"

The judge replied with an emphatic iambic: "The house belongs to them!"

The evictees in *Wells Fargo v. Epps* were a sixty-year-old woman and a tall, elderly gentleman so frail he seemed slightly transparent.

"Mr. Dorsey is claiming tenancy in the property," the bank's lawyer explained to the judge.

"You were a bona fide tenant before the foreclosure procedure started?" the judge asked the frail man. (A tenant has ninety days to vacate after a foreclosure.) Mr. Dorsey handed papers to the bailiff. The judge and the bank's lawyer mumbled over the rent receipts and leases. Something predated something else, I thought I heard. For that or other reasons the documents weren't good enough to delay the eviction.

Mrs. Epps tried another tack.

"I had been working with the mortgage company for a year for a modification. They told me I could go to NACA"—the Neighborhood Assistance Corporation of America is a private organization whose counselors help homeowners negotiate with their mortgage servicers—"but two weeks later they took the property."

"If someone misled you," the judge said, cutting her off, "you may have a cause of action in *another* court. But *not* in *this* court." And once again he uttered that iambic finality: "The house belongs to them."

Mrs. Epps shoved her papers into her purse and headed toward the hallway. She still had some will in her walk, but Mr. Dorsey moved like a wraith.

I was at the courthouse to meet a blind woman in a wheelchair who was also losing her home. A Legal Aid lawyer had already set up the interview. All I could do was pursue this Mrs. Epps into the hallway to see if I could meet her later.

"I fell behind to bury my son," she explained as soon as I introduced myself. "He was killed in an unsolved murder . . . I called them [the mortgage company] and said, 'I have to bury my child; I need two months. Will you work with me?' They said . . ."

I asked if we could meet for lunch, but Mrs. Epps, a home health aide, was going straight back to her patient. She suggested that we meet at the Mexicali Rose in Oakland that evening.

"My Head Feels Like a Pincushion"

When I arrived at the restaurant, Alice Epps was already seated. Alone in a booth for four, she looked small, but she reinflated when we started to talk.

"I can't believe what happened today . . . Put 'em on a separate plate," she told the waiter when I said I'd skip the French fries that come with the pork chops and rice and beans. "I'll take 'em home."

The word "home" seemed to remind Mrs. Epps about the imminent visit from the sheriff and the four floors of furnishings waiting there. "I hear they hold your things ten days before they dump 'em."

Mr. Dorsey was also waiting back home for her. "I phoned him to come eat with us. He said he felt too weak to get off the bed." Mr. Dorsey is a diabetic. The county pays Mrs. Epps to care for him a few hours a week. By a separate arrangement, she's also his landlady.

In her agitation Alice began telling me about the many mortgage "shams"—that was a word she used frequently—that she'd encountered. Mrs. Epps had bought her house in Richmond for $35,000 in 1972. By the late 1980s she'd paid off her mortgage and owned the house free and clear. During the housing boom Alice got letters and almost daily phone calls offering her first tens of thousands and then hundreds of thousands of dollars in refinance loans against the increased value of her home. She ignored them until her daughter started college.

"I saw what she was paying for rent, and I said, 'Eight hundred dollars a month!' You could be paying off a house note for that money." Meanwhile, her married son was renting next door. "I was so comfortable with my child next door to me." This was the son who was killed. So Alice made the fateful decision to leverage her primary asset.

"I borrowed against my house and purchased the house next door for my son. I paid $22,000 to get the loan in his name, and I found a house for my daughter in Vacaville. Cost me $40,000 to get her into a house.

"It was an adjustable rate—no, they wouldn't give me a fixed rate—that started at 7.9, call it 8 percent. It was supposed to go down if I paid for two years, but instead it went up to 17 percent."

Did Mrs. Epps really believe that the interest on her adjustable rate mortgage would go down as a reward for paying on time for two years? Did the loan salesman mislead her or outright lie about how much the payments could go up when the initial or teaser rate adjusted?

Investors who bought mortgage-backed securities have won big settlements from banks because they were given fraudulent or misleading information about the riskiness of the mortgages. But it would be hard to win compensation for borrowers when the fraud (if it occurred) went on during a sales pitch with no disinterested witnesses around.

Whatever she was told, or wishfully believed, Alice, like millions of others, couldn't keep up when her adjustable rate mortgage payments rose by hundreds of dollars a month.

"When my son got killed, I called and told them I need to bury my child, I need two months. So they said I should go ahead and bury my child: 'We'll work with you.' So they offered me, what do you call them things Obama's giving?"

"A modification?"

"Yeah?"

"And you got it?!"

"Yeah, took a couple of weeks."

A couple of weeks?! Alice Epps managed to get a loan modification in a matter of weeks when a cool head like Balty Alatas couldn't wade through the paperwork in a year and a half?

"My note became $4,939, close to $5,000, per month. I worked two, three jobs at a time and paid it. One month I earned $12,000. Then I tried to get away from Litton by refinancing but . . ."

"Litton!"

"But they [a new mortgage originator] sold my mortgage right back to them [Litton]."

Suddenly I understood how she got a modification. To most underwater homeowners, the word "modification" referred to an ineffective government program meant to keep people in their houses. But there are many ways to modify the terms of a mortgage. Litton Loan Servicing is known among consumer advocates for offering mortgage modifications that fail and leave homeowners owing more than ever.

This is how that works out profitably for them: Normally, a

mortgage servicer passes along all of the interest and principal it collects to the banks or investors who own the mortgages. The servicer earns its money from regular service fees, late penalties, and special charges like the ones involved in modifications.

But a mortgage servicer normally can't offer a modification (a change in a loan's basic terms) without the consent of the loan's owner. This, as we've seen, can be hard to get. But Litton and its associates buy up delinquent or otherwise malodorous mortgages at a discount. With the original investors out of the picture, Litton is free to grant modifications in its own interest.

During the course of most Litton modifications or "trial" modifications, the homeowner's payments can consist almost entirely of fees and new interest. By offering one likely-to-fail modification after another, Litton can collect payments like Alice Epps's $4,939 a month for as long as the homeowner can pay. The company is free to raise or even lower the payments if it decides that's the best way to squeeze out a few last drops. But since almost none of the money goes to paying off the mortgage debt, the recipients of Litton modifications often wind up owing more than they would have if they'd never been granted the favor. When they've paid all they can, they lose the house.

Litton had been leading people in poor neighborhoods through this Kafkaesque modification maze well before the Great Recession. After the crash it came under press scrutiny because it had been acquired by Goldman Sachs. The calm, cool, and collected *Financial Times* took a stab at describing Litton's modification procedures in a story of June 16, 2010, titled "US Consumers Rage Against Goldman Unit." In its accompanying human interest feature titled " 'A Quick Fix' That Added More to Debt," the *Finan-*

cial Times's sample Litton customers are a white couple reduced to near lunacy by Litton's modification process.

Alice knew the term "modification" in connection with her Litton loan, but she had also heard about what many in her neighborhood call "Obama modifications." She pursued that angle too, or at least she'd started several times.

NACA, the organization she'd mentioned to the judge, holds traveling Save the Dream conclaves where distressed homeowners gather in places like civic centers to meet counselors who might be able to get a concession from their mortgage company right there over the phone or at least get legitimate negotiations started.

Other groups, both altruistic and not so altruistic, offer similar services. Alice had tried both kinds.

"I went to five different community agencies. I waited all day in Pittsburg [California]. But it was a sham. All those agencies getting money from the federal government saying they are helping people. They're shams and frauds. Do Obama know what's going on? So I hooked up with Help-U-Modify. They charge $3,500."

"And you paid them . . . ?"

"Thirty-five hundred dollars. Come to find out, Help-U-Modify wasn't even licensed. They was taking people's money—they're still taking people's money—but they don't do nothing. The Legal Aid told me they weren't even licensed."

"You went to Legal Aid?"

"They told me that they were too busy, had too many cases. I asked the judge today, 'Don't I get no papers?' He says, 'I'll give *them* [the bank's lawyer] a writ.' I don't even know how long I got to do anything. So I called this attorney today that I'm going to see tomorrow."

"Another lawyer?!"

"He said, 'Bring $250 with you tomorrow.' I said, 'I'm about to lose my house. I went to Legal Aid, they referred me to you.' He said, 'Nah, I want $250.'"

"Alice," I'm practically pleading, "it's too late for lawyers. You have to think about where to move."

"But the judge, he said maybe I could go to another court. That's why I called that attorney."

Alice Epps isn't stupid, but she has a way of giving things a twist, a consistent way of mishearing official or legal talk that sets her off on these wild-goose chases. That morning in court the judge said that she *might* have a case in another court if someone deliberately misled her. But here, here in his courtroom, she had lost, absolutely. It was his forceful and frustrated way of cutting this thing off. Alice heard all the words but processed them as an invitation to go to another court.

"I just can't believe this is happening to me," she said. "I been living in that house thirty-eight, forty years. What's the bank want my house for?" That was certainly a reasonable question. The streets of her neighborhood were dotted with derelict bank-owned houses.

"I'm going to the bank tomorrow myself, in person, and ask them to come out to the house or say, 'Can I tender rent till I can get my stuff out of here?' And I hope they don't tell me they can't talk to me, to go to an attorney, 'cause a lawyer in Berkeley told me . . ."

"THE HOUSE BELONGS TO THEM!" I wanted to bellow. Instead, I began asking Alice about family and friends who could help her find a temporary place to move.

"My sisters, my daughter, they don't know a thing about what happened to me today." Like Bibi San Antonio, Alice hadn't told anyone, not even her daughter, about the impending eviction. "I'm used to giving help, not getting help."

"But they'll want to help you," I said. I described how unemployed bankers, "million-dollar executives," aren't embarrassed to "network" when they need something like a job. "They call everyone they ever met. By the way, do you have e-mail? . . . Okay by phone."

I listened quietly while Alice listed relatives and old friends she could call. Each had his own economic worries at the time. "What can they do for me?"

"You can never imagine in advance what you'll hear once you start asking," I said.

"Like what?" she asked. By then I had realized how limited her lucky breaks were likely to be, but I toughed it out.

"Look, I went to court today to interview a blind woman. I needed a story, I stopped a complete stranger, and I got to you."

Then Alice really got to *me*.

"I kept saying, 'Lord, I don't know if this is good for me. I don't know what she is doing.' And I prayed about it, and then I said, 'I'll go meet her. I'll go because she is tiny. She can't do me no harm.'"

Oh, God, I can't hurt her, because I'm small. "No, I'm not going to do you any harm," I said, "but I'm not going to do you any good. That's the problem." Then I moved to Alice's side of the booth and cried because my books never do anyone any good.

Mrs. Epps said she understood because all her patients always die. "The doctor tells me it will be four months, but I'll keep 'em a year or two. That's my job, to keep 'em. But in the end, they pass."

I learned more about Alice's son that evening. He'd worked for a moving and storage company. If he were alive, he'd know how to handle the packing and where to store her things. But if he were alive, that wouldn't be necessary, because she wouldn't have paid $12,000 to bury him, so maybe this wouldn't be happening.

"I don't know how I'm going to sleep tonight," Alice said. "My head feels like a pincushion."

Mrs. Epps insisted on driving me to the bus stop because she felt it was dangerous for me to walk in the neighborhood at night. "I can't say that I'm sorry that I bought my children homes," she said, "but if I had knew what I know today, I would never have borrowed against my house."

Chapter Eleven

AN OLD-FASHIONED FORECLOSURE WITH A MODERN TWIST

The Return of Option One

Unlike Alice Epps, the blind woman I'd come to meet that day in court never tried to profit from the house price boom and instinctively kept her distance from mortgage sharks. But in some waters sharks abound.

Fifteen years earlier Eletta Robertson had been living as a renter with her own six children, three orphaned relative children, and her mentally disabled cousin Curtis. This adult cousin stood quietly behind her wheelchair wearing a four-year-old's grin except at moments when something startled him. A word from Eletta calmed him immediately.

When her landlord wanted to sell the house, Mrs. Robertson bought it as a way to keep the large family together. The landlord helpfully waited six months while Eletta worked two jobs to pay off some credit card debt. That allowed her to qualify for a decent, old-fashioned, fixed-rate mortgage.

Seven years later she had a fall at work (she'd been an aide in a children's group home) that left her in a wheelchair. The gradual blindness was diabetes related.

Before the Great Recession the most common causes of bankruptcy were job loss and catastrophic medical bills. Mrs. Robertson suffered from both. Yet she'd managed to keep current on her mortgage payments for another seven years with the help of workers' compensation. Unfortunately, she'd been transferred to California's state disability system. With its recession-slashed budget, the state didn't cover enough of the costs when Eletta had new medical bills. Mrs. Robertson fell behind on her mortgage payments and caught up a couple of times. But when a fallen tree created electricity damage, the repair bill combined with the increased medical bills put her over the line, and she went bankrupt.

She was in court that day to firm up a seven-week delay that her Legal Aid lawyer had already negotiated with the bank's lawyer. He expressed regret that all he could do was buy her a little time. Eletta responded with gratitude. It would give her time to find a place where she could keep everyone together. That's what mattered.

Outside the courthouse Mrs. Robertson answered my questions courteously because that was her nature. But she didn't have a "victim's" passion to tell her story. From her point of view, she couldn't pay her mortgage, so she lost her house. It was a misfortune, not an injustice.

Before we parted, however, she broached a topic that stirred other emotions. "May I tell you something?" And here stress came into her voice. A couple of years earlier a close relative had transferred a house into cousin Curtis's name. "They *gifted* him the property, and they was gonna *gift* it back to themselves. In the meantime, they had Curtis sign for a $318,000 mortgage."

"What?!" I exclaimed.

Eletta had become aware of it through an IRS letter about taxes

Curtis would owe. She thought that it must be an error. "Then I got his credit report, and it was right on there; he borrowed for a mortgage. So I called Option One to get that changed."

"Option One?!"

Option One is the name I asked my readers to remember. It's the loan company involved in a foreclosure that Judge Schack of Brooklyn dismissed as fishy. He noticed that the company had transferred a mortgage the day before the borrower signed for it. "Nonexistent mortgages and notes are incapable of assignment," Judge Schack wrote. With that he bought a "little guy," in this case a black hospital worker from Brooklyn, more time.

"My question," Eletta continued, "is how in the world did that go through? Curtis don't work; Curtis can't show no pay stubs; so how could they give Curtis a mortgage?"

That's a reasonable question. One innovation of the securitization craze was a mortgage that requires no proof of stated income. It's commonly called the "liar's loan." But looking at cousin Curtis, I realized that Curtis can't even lie!

Still, his signature had been accepted by someone connected with Option One. His brief foray into home ownership might have jeopardized his Supplemental Security Income payments for the rest of his life, Eletta feared. "So I had to go down to SSI and explain. What SSI did is put a restraining order against [the offending relative]. He couldn't come around Curtis for three years."

Now Eletta worried that Curtis's spurious mortgage might threaten her family again. A rental agent she'd seen the day before took $30 per adult who would be living in the house as his fee for doing credit checks. "I tried to explain to the agent that I take care of all the bills. He said not to worry, there'd be no problem as long as there was no eviction on anyone's record. But now that I think about it, they foreclosed that property. So maybe Curtis has an eviction against him."

"If it's really on his credit record," I suggested, "I bet your Legal Aid lawyer can straighten it out with a couple of phone calls. I know he really wants to help." That seemed to ease her mind.

"But I still want it to be clear," Mrs. Robertson appealed to me. "Curtis never bought a house. And that debt shouldn't be on his credit report when he leaves this world. That's not fair to him."

The Greatest Setback Since the End of Reconstruction

I hadn't thought to put black home losers in a special category. But I happened to meet two black women in foreclosure court on the same day, and the Option One–related foreclosure that Judge Schack found so questionable concerned a house owned by a black man. It isn't just coincidence that three black homeowners encountered quintessential subprime hustlers.

In the decades before the housing boom, traditional banks avoided mortgage lending in black neighborhoods. Legitimate bankers of the pre-boom era would deny drawing literal red lines around black neighborhoods. But in those days the minimal characteristic of a good loan was that the borrower be able to pay it back. Black incomes were, for reasons our good bankers might deplore, low and insecure—at least on the average.

So the inner-city lending niche was filled by just the kinds of "financiers" you would expect. Litton and Option One were among them.

But once traditional lenders figured out how to get ghetto loans rated AAA and then get them off their books, they could erase those invisible red lines and rush in. Indeed, the large regular banks were so anxious for a steady supply of subprime mortgages that they financed and/or bought the irregular lenders who already knew how to operate in those neighborhoods.

Soon you had the old ghetto lenders, now backed with seemingly unlimited new cash, offering no-money-down, interest-only, adjustable rate, balloon, and other oddly shaped mortgages to people who couldn't afford them.

Eletta Robertson was never swept up into the housing bubble. She bought her house with a traditional loan and lost it through a traditional catastrophe. She experienced the subprime frenzy via her cousin Curtis's loan.

Alice Epps, on the other hand, participated in the mania. She borrowed on the rising value of her paid-off house in order to make down payments on two more houses. If it had worked out, we'd call it leveraging. Though these women's stories are as different as their temperaments, the economic results were the same.

Eletta Robertson lost the house she'd paid on for fifteen years, and Alice Epps lost the house she'd once owned free and clear. Results have been similar for a disproportionate number of black homeowners.

In August 2010 the industry newspaper *Mortgage Servicing News* reported that nearly 8 percent of African-American families had already lost a home in the Great Recession compared with 4.5 percent of white families. The number of imminent foreclosures would soon bring the home loss up to 11 percent for black families and 17 percent for Latino families, the publication estimated.

After the Civil War a large number of freed slaves deposited their savings regularly in the Freedman's Savings Bank, many under the impression that it was connected somehow to the U.S. government. When the Freedman's Bank failed in 1874 (after the pretty great recession of 1873), it dampened a black generation's hopes to own homes, start businesses, or retire in security. It reinforced the notion that these middle-class things "just weren't meant for us."

The Freedman's Savings Bank had nineteen branches in twelve states. It was large, but it never had as much as 10 percent of American blacks as its depositors. But close to 10 percent of today's African-American mortgage holders have already lost their homes in the Great Recession. For most of these families their homes were their major or only wealth. The Great Recession has produced the greatest setback to black economic equality since the Freedman's Bank crashed. And that's just so far.

Mortgage Moralities

When the foreclosure wave first hit, conservatives blamed greedy, shortsighted borrowers. Weak people unwilling to defer gratification bought houses they couldn't afford. Liberals blamed greedy, shortsighted lenders. Cunning bankers made stupid loans because they could pass the risk to investors and the government.

I encountered quite a range of moral attitudes among borrowers and lenders. But I'm not sure how much these different personal moralities contributed to the crisis.

Borrowers like Cindi and Amanda had little choice but to pay high prices for houses; still, they hoped to profit when those prices went even higher. When prices fell instead, they sought to cut their losses in whatever way worked best for them. Like most homeowners, they felt neither gratitude nor malice toward the banks that lent them money. It's hard to feel a personal obligation when one's mortgage loan passes through so many hands. Still, a few borrowers like Eletta Robertson thought of their bank debt as a personal promise and tried to pay as long as possible.

When I arrived in California, the upright Balty Alatas planned to go on paying his mortgage, even though he couldn't. A year later he stopped paying, even though he could. This crisis is fraying our national ethic about debt. I wonder if it applies only to mortgage debt, and I wonder if the lawlessness will be lasting.

Alice Epps was trying to turn one paid-off home into three. Some might call her a good mother who tried to provide secure nests for her children by leveraging the only chunk of capital she was likely to control in her lifetime. Others might say that she tried to take advantage of loose credit and failed because she didn't have the knowledge or discipline.

To Bibi San Antonio houses are for speculation: her goal was to buy cheap and sell dear. When house prices dropped, Bibi demonstrated her own kind of morality by getting back to former customers and advising them to default right away. She felt no such loyalty to the banks that had paid her commissions.

Bibi's daughter, who loves her mother "to death," notes that her mother shares certain moral attitudes with big financiers. But as a "capitalist without capital," she'll never be "inside" enough, her daughter says, to get in on the next pyramid scheme early.

I'm not "inside" enough, myself, to generalize about big bankers and their mortgage moralities. But here's someone who is.

A CNBC program on the mortgage crisis ended by asking our former Federal Reserve chairman Alan Greenspan why no one saw the mortgage crisis coming and told the bankers, "You know what, this is going to end badly."

Greenspan answered: "It's not that they weren't aware that the risks were there; I mean, I spoke to them. It's not that the people were dumb: they knew precisely what was going on. The vast majority of them thought that they knew when to get out. It was a failure of our 'best and brightest.'"

Bibi, too, thought she knew when to get out. She understood her daughter's warnings about the bubble. She just didn't think it would burst within five years. By the Bibi San Antonio/Alan Greenspan morality, our top bankers would have earned the title "best and brightest" without quotation marks if they'd managed to dump the losses onto others in time.

Like Bibi, Greenspan's bankers didn't think of houses as places to live. Though they were allocating the nation's capital, they didn't ask how many houses are needed, where should they be built, can the people who need them afford to buy them? Their only question was, how many more of these mortgages can we sell to investors? The investors in turn were asking, "How much more of this cash can I safely unload?"

This wild mortgage lending wasn't dictated by masses of poor people storming the banks demanding credit. It was fueled by a relatively few people with large piles of money that desperately needed to be invested. Hedge fund owners, pension fund managers, and European bankers are among the folks who bought mortgage-backed securities. But like others charged with great piles of cash to invest, they can reasonably blame the money itself.

You and I may not be used to thinking of big piles of money as a problem, but they can exert unbearable pressure. Feckless borrowers and greedy bankers we have always with us. It's the piles of money they lend and borrow that expand, change shape, and sometimes become inordinately demanding. These incorporeal and amoral wads of capital exerted pressures that led to the Great Recession.

III: OUR SAVINGS

Chapter Twelve

THREE INVESTORS

I began this book by contacting people who'd suffered recession-related losses. We've already met people who lost jobs and houses. We're about to meet people who saw their investments drop by as much as half in the first few months of the recession.

That had to be terrifying, especially to a generation that had been encouraged by government tax exemptions to turn what they thought of as retirement savings over to investment brokers. But unlike those who lost jobs and homes, many investors have caught up or even come out ahead—at least temporarily.

The investors I'm about to introduce you to are nice people. The hard-nosed, big-time Wall Street guys depicted in books and movies don't have time to waste with me.

Yet nice and small as my investors are, they helped me understand how piles of money can exert pressure that leads to financial crazes as stupid as the subprime mortgage mania.

"Am I Sitting Here Watching My Blood Dribble Out?"

Henrietta Center is a bossy old woman. "Where's your helmet?!" are the first words she ever said to me.

I was locking my bike in front of her apartment complex. I often go there to visit a friend, and Henrietta remembered seeing me arrive helmeted in the past. I explained that I'd been in a rush when I left and couldn't find it.

"When do you think you crack your skull open?" she asked. "When you're rushing."

I had to admit she was right. From then on we exchanged a few words whenever I saw her sitting outside. She sometimes let me help her into the elevator with her shopping wagon. "Not that I need help—yet. But I'll get there."

Henrietta, still tall and erect in her late eighties, always had advice for me. When she saw a cake box in my bicycle basket, she said, "Their stuff is overpriced; they sell it half off after four." When she saw that I'd let my hair go white, she said, "What do you want to look like me for?" She even had advice for me to convey to the friend I visited—presumptuous but astute advice about a man she had recently started dating.

Then, one day, soon after the crash, I saw her at the mailboxes, and instead of assaulting me with advice, she let me walk her to her door and asked me in.

"Could you please stay while I open this?" she said. The word "please" coming from Henrietta was a piteous surrender.

I sat where she pointed while she opened an extra-wide envelope and scanned its contents.

"Do I look like someone who just lost $80,000?" she said, passing over her brokerage statement. Henrietta's bottom line had gone down year to date by almost 40 percent.

It had been going down since "the Lehman Brothers thing," she told me. She'd called "the people that have my IRA"—she didn't know the name of anyone at the brokerage house—and reached someone who told her not to panic. She showed the statement to a nephew and heir whom she trusted in these matters, and he confirmed that the investments were basically sound and advised her to wait it out.

"But they don't remember the Depression," she said. "My nephew says it's different now, but he didn't live through it."

Later I learned that Henrietta had been set to go to college (not so common for a girl in the 1930s) until her father "lost everything" in the Depression. Instead, she went to work straight out of high school and held a series of increasingly responsible jobs with small firms in New York's flower district.

Fifty-five years later, still single, she retired on her Social Security and a small pension. These cover her modest living expenses. "The account" (her IRA) was inviolably set aside for home care. She even knew whom she would hire when the time came.

A Nepalese woman had nursed her after an earlier operation, and they hit it off. Since then, Henrietta has found the woman a lot of clients who paid her more than what she would take home through an agency.

"She calls me her manager," Henrietta said, almost cheerful for a moment. "She'll quit any other job to work for me when the time comes." Then she remembered. "But she can't work for nothing. What if this"—she held up the brokerage statement—"what if it keeps going down?"

Henrietta asked me several times what would happen, what should she do? She was almost viscerally pulled in two directions. On one hand, maybe things *were* different. She didn't want to be "an ignorant old woman who pulls my money out in a panic." But she also didn't want to be "a gullible old woman who listened to the crap some thirty-year-old kid tells the small-timers."

When her fear subsided for a moment, her mind would turn to the general situation. She'd heard on CNBC, she said, that $2 trillion or $22 trillion or maybe it was $200 trillion had already been wiped out in the crisis. "But what happens to all the stuff we could have bought with that money?" A profound question.

Then she'd remember her personal situation again, and I could almost feel her stomach drop and see the weakness spread into her limbs. "They tell me it's different today, things are insured, the worst thing you can do is panic. So, okay, it's not jump-out-the-window time. But just look"—she gestures again to her bottom line—"if this goes down by another 40 percent, what will happen to me? Am I sitting here watching my blood dribble out?"

Millions of other retirees found their portfolios falling rapidly too. Like Henrietta, many people with individual retirement accounts and 401(k)s had simply checked off boxes on forms they got through their employers. Under the management of brokerage firms that they hadn't chosen, their money grew far more than it would have if they had put it into insured bank accounts. Yet they seemed to have only the vaguest understanding that they were not savers or old-fashioned pensioners but investors. During the week of the crash I met a man on a bus who reminded the people around him about 1930s movies where "a guy in a top hat grabs the telephone mouthpiece and yells, 'Sell! Sell!' But I don't know who to call!" I imagine he eventually reached someone who advised him not to panic.

Of course many professionals representing banks, insurance companies, corporations, pension funds, and really wealthy individuals (that is, the investors who control the overwhelming bulk of securities) must have ignored such advice, or the markets wouldn't have plunged. But millions of others stood paralyzed like the proverbial deer in the headlights while their portfolio wealth declined 30 to 50 percent.

I'm going to leave Henrietta frozen like that for a while and talk to a couple of other modest investors in their later years.

"If You Give It Away, You Don't Have It"

An author I know heard that I was interviewing recession victims. She herself had been helped over a rough period by a blue-blooded and generous woman who now might qualify as a victim.

My writer acquaintance had been living in the suburbs when her husband suddenly died, leaving a messy will. His children by an earlier marriage claimed the house; they even had the electricity turned off. Perhaps the author had some legal recourse, but this wasn't the time in her life for a draining battle. She'd just gotten a book contract and wanted to get on with it.

At that moment Prudence invited the writer to move to her Manhattan apartment, explaining the modest rent by saying that they would "share" the place until Prudence sold it. But Prudence made only occasional trips to Manhattan from her Massachusetts home. Not only that, but at the height of the real estate boom Prudence postponed selling the apartment for the full two years that it took the writer to finish her book. Then, and then only, did she put the place on the market. Fortunately, it sold within a week because the housing bubble was already quietly deflating.

Prudence put her half a million dollars from the apartment sale into building a new wing on her Massachusetts house, outfitted for her old age "but so stylishly," my writer friend said, "that you don't notice the grab bars, wide doors to fit a wheelchair, special bathtub for codgers."

The first use of the new wing was another act of benevolence. When Sara, a truly penniless writer, began suffering from a lung disease, a regular cleaning woman appeared to keep her apartment dust-free. When the disease advanced to the point that Sara needed oxygen and could no longer walk the stairs to her own apartment, Prudence transported her to the codger wing, where she sheltered and fed her with such self-effacing care that Sara was able to work there for six months.

Then came the financial crash, and suddenly, according to my author informant, "Pru's financially savvy son tells her that her base expenses—taxes, maintenance of house and sixty acres, heat, car, et cetera—are more than her income, which is now down to nothing. Everything she spends is coming out of capital. Now she's trying to rent half the house to help pay for expenses.

"She was always the most generous landlady, always arriving with lovely stuff from the bakery or a book she thought I'd like. Now she's eking it out. I know you're discreet about all this. If it fits what you're doing, I can ask Prudence if she'd talk to you."

Frankly, I hadn't envisaged the typical recession victim as "eking it out" on sixty acres in one of the wealthiest communities on the Eastern Seaboard. But to someone of inherited wealth, having to "dip into capital" is bound to be distressing. Besides, I was curious.

Prudence picked me up at the train in an old station wagon. She was wearing gardening boots and loose clothing that could pass for pajamas. Her face beamed with cream, butter, and the benevolence she was known for.

The house was as lovely as I'd heard—the new wing airy and inviting, the old wing cozy and inviting. Both blended unobtrusively into the New England woodland that surrounded the house. I complimented Pru on the renovation.

The original plan, she explained, was to be able to offer the old wing as a free home to some person or family who would help her when she became less self-sufficient. "Someone to bring hot meals to me the way I did for Sara." But because of the stock market crash, the house would now have to become income producing. She'd already had a couple of short-term rentals.

While Pru bustled to set out a cold lunch (amid apologies), I looked around. On one wall I noticed a set of Audubon prints, on another, a group of dark, 1830s-style portraits. "Your ancestors?" I joked about the stiff-collared fellows in their gilt frames.

"This one fought in the Revolution and became a banker. This one we don't know that much about, except he doesn't seem to have been a nice person. And Thomas W. was a lawyer and banker in Philadelphia. That's his fire bucket." She pointed to a corner of the room.

It turns out that one side of Pru's family came over on the *Mayflower* and the other was sent to help govern the Massachusetts Bay Colony. I looked again at the old bucket in the corner and realized that a lot of what I thought of as flea-market treasures scattered around must be family heirlooms.

As for the Audubons, one of her ex-husband's forefathers (they were from a richer and newer old family) subscribed to the original set in the nineteenth century. "I think you'll enjoy this detail," Pru said, and described how her husband's generation divided them up. "They dealt them out facedown like playing cards, one for you, one for you, one for you. Seventeen each, I think. These"—she pointed to the long-legged birds on the wall—"are the ones we got. My husband left them with me in exchange for the contents of the wine cellar."

After lunch we moved ahead another hundred years. I asked Pru about her parents, and she brought out the 1930s housewarming album. Their estate looked out over Long Island Sound, and I could almost hear the waves under the orchestra as guests danced beneath hanging lanterns.

"In the photos my father looks so happy and confident, my mother so beautiful. Look at them greeting the guests. It's like a Fred Astaire movie."

"Like the Great Gatsby!" I said, staring at the men in evening dress and the women with Erté gowns and marcelled hair.

"Grandfather started X [a company whose name you will certainly know], and it was a family firm till it merged with Y [you'll know that name too]. Father was a director. But he opposed the merger so strongly that he left the company and sold all the stock in the middle of the Depression. Then there were his own schemes." My husband recognized Pru's father's name in connection with a warplane he developed but couldn't sell to the government.

"At the height of his financial panic we were living on a private beach of over a mile in a huge house with horrendous expenses, and Father started running around the mansion turning off the lights. With personalities like ours, reality doesn't always sink in quickly enough.

"By the time I was eight or nine, all that"—she gestured to the album—"was over. But wherever we lived, the housewarming album was always on the piano. It was the Shangri-La of happy marriage and great prosperity."

Now we were up to the present, and I thought it would be uncomfortable for Prudence to talk about her own finances. In fact, it was, but she was determined to learn how.

"When I grew up, it was normal to be rich and 'we don't talk about money.' Women certainly don't. That's why Sara and I decided that we will always talk about money and use the real numbers. It was hard at first, like using dirty words."

Hard as it was, Pru did her best to tell me how she lived before the crash and how she lives now in real numbers.

"Before the crash I took $2,500 a month, and if I needed to paint the house—that was $20,000—then I just ask them to sell something."

"Them" was a firm created in the nineteenth century to handle her family's investments. It would accommodate Pru's onetime expenditures by selling some equities. A frequent category of one-time expenditure was purchases from local artists or the kinds of benevolences that I'd heard about. Pru didn't seem to engage in the formal charity that gets one's name on letterheads. In her own words, she simply "saw what needed to be done and did it."

"One year I spent $30,000, well, almost $40,000 on charity," she admitted. "But in the nineties my money in the stock market tripled. So you could give it away, and it would replenish itself.

"By 2007, I realized that things weren't going up by 30 percent anymore. Before I deposited the money from selling the apartment, I had about . . ."

Pru tried sincerely to come up with her net worth. She'd remember things like the stocks her father-in-law handed her personally over the years—then couldn't recall whether they'd been sold or not. As she said, she was brought up not to talk or think about money. But by her best effort she came up with a figure of about $600,000.

I suspect she'd find other bits of wealth tucked away here and there if she looked. Pru never, for instance, considered the cash value of the Audubons, the ancestors, or the first-edition books she'd pick up usually meant for some acquaintance who might like them.

"But then," she recalled, "between September '08 and November '08, it dropped down to under $400,000. By the speed it was dropping, I realized that I was looking into the abyss."

"So what did you do?" I asked.

"I quickly canceled my cell phone and all my newspaper and magazine subscriptions."

I let out a laugh but swallowed it. "I'm sorry, I was just thinking about your father and the lights."

In her own panic she phoned her son to help her get a grip on her finances.

"My son told me that I did not have an 'income' as in a Jane Austen novel. I had a finite amount of money. And if I kept spending the way I was spending, then in three years I would have to sell the house and go live in an apartment.

"He was furious that I had made no investments for steady income. What I didn't realize was that everything I had was in stocks. But I can't sell while the market is down like this. If I did that, I'd have to take a permanent loss." As her father had done.

"My son made a point of letting me know that he and his partner—he'd started some companies in Japan—had problems too. He couldn't be in a position of bailing me out, but he was willing to put in a lot of work helping me in my reformation."

So Pru and her son got serious about budget cuts.

"I decided to mow only half the lawn and just make pathways through the rest." The gardeners would now come every *other* week. Pru also decreased the cleaning woman's hours. "I asked if she wanted me to find her other customers, but she said she was fully booked. That made it easier."

Other cuts were more difficult. "I believe in supporting the local economy, and the pharmacist was already hurting. But the stock market crash hit just as I fell into the Medicare gap. I was spending over $500 a month on drugs . . . One anticancer drug was $350 a month. I asked my doctors did I really have to take it, and they said yes, if I didn't want to have cancer.

"So in January I switched all my prescriptions to a mail-order plan where you get three months at a time. And I've never gone back to the pharmacy," she said with remorse. "I've always believed it's important to bring your business where it helps. But this is the sort of impulse that has been slapped out of me."

Less than a year later I was in Pru's home with my husband as a weekend guest.

"Wow, white tea!" I cried when I spotted the large silver bags from Upton. I was merely thinking about the different teas I'd get to try, but Pru took it as a comment on her profligacy.

"I was so tired of being penurious," she apologized. "The stocks are up, so life can go back to normal in little things."

"So what are you back to spending on?" I asked, pulling out my notebook. What a bore I am. Money is Pru's least favorite topic, and I was there on a social visit. Still, she obliged me by listing some recent indulgences.

Her home was going to be on a house tour for a local charity, so she'd fixed the lightning rods. "They were actually falling over. We pulled out the copper and reused it, but it was still $4,000."

She'd also refinished two silver pieces—"one of my father's racing trophies and a candy dish.

"The man I brought it to said the dish was Russian, 1883. He turned it over and recognized the name of the maker from the St. Petersburg area. And the sailing trophy was Tiffany's, but it wasn't from the 1930s—that's when my father raced—it was probably made in the 1880s. He said they mass ordered them and put dates on later.

"It was such a delight to listen to his esoteric information that I never even thought to ask what it would cost. The bill was $640. The Upton's tea order came to $180."

My husband asked if items of that size could really affect her overall security.

"They most certainly do," she said. "When those bills came, I had to take money out of capital and put it in the checking account."

In Pru's family circles "dipping into capital" was a sign of moral weakness and often imminent ruin. "I must train myself to always ask, 'How much will it cost?'"

————

At the start of most dinners Prudence says the same brief blessing: "Thank you for food, thank you for friends, and make us mindful of the needs of others." When I admired that last clause, she said that she'd picked it up from a retired minister friend. "But with the recession he switched to 'make us mindful of the poor.'"

"I don't like that as much," I said.

"Me neither," Pru agreed. "I told him I felt singled out now that I'm about to be poor myself. He's changed it back."

Does Pru still worry that she's about to be poor? She's too mindful of the needs of others and the real conditions of other lives to call herself poor. What she answers instead is "I learned from the crash that my money is finite."

"Does that mean no more art and charity?" I asked.

"Before, the money I was giving away was being replaced like magic by the stock market," she answered. "Now I know, like that stingy husband of mine, that if you give it away, you don't have it."

Brenda Takes Charge of Her Portfolio

Brenda Staark and I bonded in jail when we did ten days for our part in the Free Speech Movement sit-in in Berkeley. (Mario Savio and all that.) Since then, we've found ourselves on different coasts and in different circles. But whenever I catch up with her, I'm always surprised.

One time she picked me up in L.A. in a pink convertible—with a tiny dog riding next to her. Early in the computer age Brenda migrated to Silicon Valley to sell business computers and gradually moved up to more high-tech products. One of her last jobs was as a saleswoman for a huge (and to me scary) military contractor. To make sales, she had to visit civilian companies and figure out how they could use nonlethal adaptations of programs her employers developed for efficient killing. How did she learn enough to do that? I wonder.

Since Brenda keeps up with such a variety of people, I called to ask if she knew anyone who'd been affected by the recession. "Me," she answered, so I started to take notes.

While she'd worked in Silicon Valley, Brenda had managed her IRA portfolio herself. "I knew which companies were building new buildings, buying thousands of computers. I had to see their budgets in order to take their orders, so I knew which of the dot-coms were real and which were mirages."

Over the course of the 1980s and into the 1990s her investments in technology stocks grew by over 500 percent, she says, and what's more, she got out before the dot-com bubble burst.

My friend Brenda has a lot of interests, so as soon as she felt she had enough money for the rest of her life, she retired. "I was traveling, going to the theater, I ate all organic foods, took the kids on trips. Yes, I lived well. But since I was no longer an 'insider,' I turned my portfolio over to a financial manager."

When the Great Recession hit, she too was advised not to panic. Social Security and a safe annuity provided half her monthly income, so at first she watched, waited, and cut her discretionary spending. For instance, she changed the weekly lunch with her son from a restaurant meal to a picnic. "We still had our special time together."

To get some new money coming in, Brenda looked for work as a nanny and quickly found more hours than she wanted. "There are still wealthy people in this town, and they want someone who speaks English well and is like them. I always get top dollar," she assured me and then thought about the other side of that coin. "I guess some people must be losing their jobs because people like me are taking them."

(A *Washington Post* article of June 13, 2009, supports Brenda's conjecture with its headline "Nannies No Longer Rule the Roost: Parents Regain Economic Power to Be Picky in Hiring Help." According to the head of a nanny agency whom the *Post* interviewed, clients now freely express their preference for "college-educated, American" nannies. And they're easy to find. The nannies interviewed found their pay and working conditions worsening.)

"When the market got to the point where I had lost 40 percent of my life's savings, I said to my manager, 'This has got me scared,' and he said, 'It always goes down in the spring and will go back up.'"

At that point Brenda took back the active management of her portfolio. She studied intensively with a trader-mentor and read for about four hours each morning. When she was finally ready, she liquidated her mutual fund holdings entirely in order to begin investing in gold.

"I track the Dow, the S&P, spot gold, silver, crude oil, and copper prices every day and enter them on my own special spreadsheet. In January, when gold went down to eight hundred something dollars an ounce, I made my first purchase."

Brenda's plan was to shift about 10 percent of her worth into gold and silver and to buy dividend-yielding blue-chip shares while they were down.

I never felt I could ask my old friend how much money she had before the crash, how much she lost, or exactly how much she has now. But if she followed her gold, silver, and depressed blue chips strategy, Brenda should have come out of the crisis well ahead.

One early hint of her improving fortunes is that she was soon accepting only nanny jobs that fit into her schedule without breaking up the day. I suspect she only worked those few hours in order to keep a bit of warm baby in her life. But when I congratulated her recently on her gold strategy—the price had more than doubled—she reminded me that so far it's still only paper gains.

By the summer of 2009, Henrietta's portfolio hadn't fully recovered, but she was only down by about $20,000. That should have been distressing to someone who buys day-old bread. But for Henrietta there's no connection between the money she lives on and "the account."

In some ways, Henrietta, the poorest of my three investors, adhered most closely to the rule of the very rich. She never went into capital. She lives off her Social Security and small pension. There's little way she could have cut that spending when her portfolio went down, and there's no way she'd dip into it when it goes back up.

At this point in the recovery she felt sure that she could pay for a couple of years of home help—as long as that didn't include an overly extended period of round-the-clock care. Besides, the market was still going up. That left her confident enough to start giving me advice again.

She suggested that I interview her future caretaker's sister about the recession. Under Henrietta's management the caretaker herself had remained steadily employed throughout the downturn. But her sister, a housekeeper/nanny for a family in Brooklyn, had been laid off when the husband of the family took big cuts at his "hotshot" job.

As their situation stabilized, the family called the housekeeper back, but because of changes in their work schedules they now needed some weekend hours. "But they're paying her the same!" Henrietta said indignantly.

According to Henrietta, the sister was scared because she knew so many other unemployed Nepalese they could hire. "I can't make those women understand that if they called her back when they could hire someone new, that's the time to ask for a raise."

"You should manage both sisters," I said.

In fact, Henrietta had already offered to call the Brooklyn brownstoners. Her plan was to say that she was interested in hiring their housekeeper herself and to ask if they could possibly work out some time sharing. By Henrietta's theory of supply and demand, interest from another employer could only help. "But they're so scared they won't even give me the number."

I suggested that the sister might be illegal.

"So what? They need her!" Henrietta argued.

I started to explain about twenty-four million unemployed, forty years of downward pressure on wages. "The problem is . . ."

"The problem is that these women are idiots!" Henrietta said. Yet she'll go on hustling up better-paying jobs for them, I know. It was good to see her back in form.

"You Have to Put It Somewhere"

Henrietta, Prudence, and Brenda aren't the only individual investors who saw their portfolios reinflate. Merrill Lynch issues an annual *World Wealth Report*, which tracks high-net-worth individuals (HNWIs) and ultra-high-net-worth individuals (UHNWIs). The highs are worth over $1 million and the ultra-highs over $30 million. That doesn't include their houses, boats, art collections, jewels, and so on. It only refers to the portfolio wealth that Merrill might invest for them if it got their accounts to manage.

At the start of the Great Recession, "world wealth" took a dive. But in the two years following the crash, the numbers of highs and ultra-highs around the globe rebounded—most dramatically in the United States. The main factor in that comeback was the rise in stock prices. When stock prices went down, many individual portfolios dipped under those $1 million and $30 million marks. But as investors regained their "risk appetite" (to use a financial-page phrase) and got back into the stock market, share prices rose, and bottom lines floated back up.

But why in the world did investors bid stock prices back up when sales at the companies whose shares they were buying were still down? Our three retirees may be relatively small and unsophisticated investors, but they answered that question in exactly the same way as their ultra-high-net-worth brethren.

When Pru told me that her portfolio had more or less recovered, I assumed she would then transfer some money out of the stock market and into the safer, interest-yielding investments that her son thought appropriate.

"We should have done that before the crash," Prudence said,

"but now no one is offering much interest. And my son says that the investments themselves do look very good, so . . ." Prudence trailed off, suggesting her helplessness to do anything but what her family brokers suggested. "You have to keep your money somewhere," she apologized.

Brenda had dumped all of her stock market mutual funds after the crash. "You can't find out what fund managers are buying, so you just have to trust them—which I don't anymore." Now she was buying gold whenever it went down.

"My other strategy is high-dividend stocks. This is what I do. When I get the dividend, it goes into a cash account. I let the cash build up, and when the market dips, I buy more stock. I spend several hours each day doing my research, and when there's a scare like a few weeks ago, I'm ready with my list—the down triggers my buy order."

"Weren't you afraid?" The scare she referred to was so volatile that it made seasoned traders nauseous.

"The economy is in the shits," Brenda answered, "but banks and mortgage companies are loaded with cash, and they pass it back. Some regular corporations are good buys too if you look at their price-earnings ratios. People are selling because of political crises and debt fears. But frankly, as long as companies keep paying me those 15 percent dividends, I don't care if their stock drops to nothing."

"Fifteen percent?!" I was shocked.

"I have one at 18 percent. Most are around 9 percent, but it all adds up."

So Brenda was taking dividends from companies that couldn't find profitable uses for money in their own line of business and using the money to buy more stocks in those companies.

"Do you think it's right to be in the stock market?" I asked.

"The current run-up of the market is a bubble," Brenda answered. "It's based on people having billions of dollars that they need to invest, not on the prospects of the companies they're investing in. But I still see opportunities, so I'm in the market."

"Well, if your money is inflating another bubble, then, I mean . . ." I didn't intend to attack my friend's ethics, but I finally managed to say, "I'm not asking is it *safe* to be in the stock market; I'm asking do you think it's *right*?"

"Do I think it's productive? No. Am I going to take advantage of it? Yes."

Much of Henrietta's money also stayed in equities. When her portfolio was down by only a few thousand dollars, I decided it was my turn to give her advice. She's almost ninety and has what she thinks she needs for home care, so I suggested that she preserve her principal even if she earned no return.

"Is it such a sin to keep your money in an insured bank account?!" I asked, adopting her own Socratic style of argument.

"Do you know what a bank pays?" she countered. "Under 1 percent. My broker"—she now knows a name there—"says it doesn't even keep pace with inflation."

After a particularly scary stock market week, I returned to the argument. "What if it drops again just when you need the money?" Having made a decision, Henrietta didn't want to endure more doubt. She cut me off with the ultimate financial wisdom: "You have to put it somewhere."

"If We Had a Market on Mars . . ."

Investors with a lot more savvy and a lot more money than my three ladies were saying the same thing.

In 2011, Terry Gross of the NPR show *Fresh Air* interviewed the renowned hedge fund "quant," or quantitative analyst, Ed Thorp. She introduced him as the mathematician who basically invented card counting at blackjack tables and went on to develop the financial equivalents—mathematical formulas for trading mortgage derivatives and credit-default swaps.

"Things that were basically behind the market collapse of 2008," Terry said. Her guest didn't demur.

Thorp told Terry that the hedge fund industry had gone back to its risky practices once it seemed that there wasn't going to be significant derivatives regulations anytime soon.

With her characteristic directness Terry asked, "So how's that affecting how much you want to have invested in the market?"

"Well, it's tough," Thorp answered. "The question is, you know, *where do you go*? There's—we only have one world we live in. If we had a market on Mars, you might think about going there. But . . ."

So a man who thinks in billions is also saying, "You have to put it somewhere."

That "have to" is even more imperative for a financial institution than an individual investor. Whoever pays interest has to earn interest. A bank can't keep your money in the bank. Even during a recession it has to put your money somewhere.

Goldman Sachs has emerged from past recessions in good shape because of its greatly admired acumen at buying up distressed assets, including bad debts, excess shopping malls, discounted mortgages left after a bust. (Buying Litton was supposed to aid with that strategy.)

But according to a front-page story in the *Financial Times* on February 6, 2011, that was hard in this recovery even for Goldman:

> Goldman Sachs' attempt to spend some of its $170bn excess capital on distressed assets . . . is being hampered by a prolonged rebound in risk appetite that has lifted prices on many would-be bargains . . .
>
> The rapid return of risk appetite . . . has left a number of [other] distressed assets funds bereft of opportunities.

What, then, would Goldman Sachs do with its "excess capital"? When its chief financial officer was asked that question, he said, "Our number one choice will be to find opportunities to use the capital profitably, and if not we would probably give some more back [to shareholders]."

Companies give money back to shareholders through dividends or stock buybacks. At that point it becomes the problem of people like Pru, Brenda, Henrietta, and much larger investors to figure out what to do with it.

In theory, these big returns should mean that my three investors have bigger heaps of capital to finance businesses that will produce goods and services while generating jobs and more profit to reinvest in more production. That's what capital not only is supposed to do but has actually done at certain times in history. I know the three women would like to use their wealth to create new business and employment. Why is it so hard for them to do that now?

Before I answer that question and think about how we'll emerge from the Great Recession, I'd like to introduce an investor who lost *all* his money and hasn't gotten a penny back yet. Being penniless was so new to him that he has some refreshing takes on the subject.

Chapter Thirteen

RICH OR POOR, IT'S GOOD TO HAVE MONEY

"Completely Vulnerable"

Richard Bey (his real name) is a longtime radio and TV talk show host who invented some of the best and worst features of the genre. (You can see him playing himself, the archetypal TV host, in the Sacha Baron Cohen movie *Brüno*.)

Over the years Bey had earned as much as $1 million a year in broadcasting. But when the recession started, he had quit an early morning show to concentrate on the child in his life, the eleven-year-old son of a former girlfriend. "He was experiencing serious issues in school, and his home support system couldn't deal with them at the time."

Money would be no immediate concern since Richard had sold his river-view apartment—"same building as Al Pacino," he volunteered—in 2005 at the height of the market. He added this windfall to the rest of his savings, which he kept in a fund run by a boyhood friend from Far Rockaway High School. As it happens, Bernie Madoff went to school there too.

But Richard's friend Bill is no Madoff. When the fund crashed, Bill wound up in the hospital with Richard consoling him. Another of the fund's executives tried to commit suicide on the Long Island

Rail Road tracks but apparently changed his mind and wound up losing only an arm and a lung. Richard feels certain that his friend Bill never actually stole from his investors, but the fund's finances are still murky.

What's definitely known is that a couple of real estate deals went bad and a German bank was defrauded. Then one bank after another froze all the money left in the fund's accounts.

Investors learned by e-mail, from a new set of managers, that all disbursements were canceled (Bey had been drawing out $8,000 a month while he wasn't working) and all funds were frozen till things could be straightened out.

When he learned that he couldn't get at his money, Richard went to the nearest ATM and found, he said, "I had $3.29 in my bank account. I had $200 in my wallet. Without a job, without income, that was all the money I had in the world. And I had just had $8,000 of oral surgery that I put on my credit card.

"At that moment I looked at the other people walking down the street. 'They can get where they need to go. But I can't buy a MetroCard. I can't put gas in the car.' *I was completely vulnerable*." Everyone without enough money to live for the rest of his life is vulnerable that way. But Richard was the first person who said this to me.

"Fortunately, I have friends. One old friend from Yale Drama School is an Obie Award–winning actress, but now she only earns $27,000 a year as a proofreader. She offered me a $1,000 loan.

"I said, 'I can't do that.'

"She said, 'Richard, all your life you've done things for your friends. You take us to dinner; you paid for Broadway shows.' But that's how I enjoy myself, going to dinner with my actor friends and talking about shows we just saw. I did that for myself. Besides, I hate to owe credit cards; I hate to owe friends. It's not in my nature to borrow."

Nevertheless, Richard took her $1,000. "We all thought the money would unfreeze in a few weeks," he explained. But because he disliked borrowing, he also raised emergency cash by selling things.

"Everything I owned became an asset—my mother's jewelry, my father's coins. I had a comic book collection of *Spider-Man* and *Iron Man*. I'd saved them for forty years, but with only a few dollars left in my wallet, they became disposable. I tried to evaluate them on the Internet, but were they in 'good' condition or 'fair' condition? Would a creased cover page knock $100 off the price? As I looked at each cover, I swear I remembered the moment when I slipped it off the rack and paid twelve cents at Milty's Candy Store.

"Eventually, I sold twenty comic books for $300 at Midtown Comics. I felt like a fool selling them that cheaply, but my wallet was once again stuffed with twenties. Later I sold the lithograph I had on my wall for fifteen years. I got $4,000. I paid $5,000. But that wasn't as painful as the comic books. After that I sold my mother's jewelry, but I still had the Liberty quarters and Indian head nickels my father had left us."

"Richard," I couldn't help asking, "didn't you ever think of the risk of having all your money in one fund?"

"Yes, Barbara, I did think about it," he said in answer to my annoying question. "In fact, I can't tell you how many times I thought of taking a chunk out of the fund for the security. But Bill made it so convenient for his investors."

Richard also wanted me to understand why it took him a while to grasp his new situation and make long-term changes.

"My rent was $4,600 a month. I had a beautiful two-bedroom. One room was fixed up for the child. That was essential. So I paid the rent by borrowing against credit cards. It didn't seem like such a bad idea, because I was expecting to pay back the loans in full as soon as the money was unfrozen. At that point they said June, so no more than two months.

"Besides, I figured that something would turn up. In my life it always has whenever I needed it. And it *did*. A friend of mine knew someone who was starting an Internet television talk network. Al Sharpton was going to be on it, Bob Grant, Curtis Sliwa. Most of the hosts were either working for free or simulcasting current radio shows. My friend suggested that with my experience and notoriety I could ask for a small salary, and I did. Six hundred dollars a week. Half the rent," he said, shrugging. "But I was working."

Many performers would be too proud or too stunned to make a quick compromise like that. But Richard, who'd had nationally syndicated TV shows, didn't worry who thought of him as a has-been, or how he'd explain it to himself. He jumped into the Internet show with his full heart.

"For the rest of the summer"—at this point the money would unfreeze in September—"I paid my debts as near the penalty dates as possible. Every Friday, I deposited my paycheck, calculated when it would clear, figured when each credit card payment had to be deducted, and double-checked my balance at the ATM. One mistake and I would face a default interest rate of 29.5 percent. I was walking on financial thin ice and finally . . .

"One Friday, I deposited my check inside, then walked out to the ATM, and the screen said negative balance. An American Express card payment of $800 was about to be withdrawn the next day. Chase must have made a mistake. I raced back into the bank to find a manager.

"When he looked at his screen, he saw that an employment check from five weeks earlier had just been reclassified as bounced. Well, five weeks before that TD Bank merged with somebody or other, and there was some computer problem during the switchover, and they stopped all the checks issued that day. Now, five weeks later, they were retrieving that stopped check from my funds. 'How can you take my money back? I thought once a check cleared, it cleared.'

"The manager explained that there were new rules, that banks had to clear checks faster now, that it was just blips, not actual money they'd move to me. But those 'just blips' left me an *actual* $800 short for American Express the next day.

"It was 2:00 p.m., and Chase would close at 6:00. I had less than four hours to come up with $800, and it had to be cash!

"I called that same friend from Yale. She worked from home, so I could count on her to be available. She said she would meet me at the bank at 3:00 p.m. and withdraw the money from her ATM. I jumped on the subway and met her on the Upper West Side. But it turned out her ATM limit was $500. I was three hundred short.

"I still had my father's coin collection. I ran home, grabbed it, and headed over to Stack's on West Fifty-seventh Street. The owner lit up when he saw me. 'Oh, I used to watch your show all the time. You gave me a lot of good laughs.' I explained my situation as he looked over the coins. He told me that in consideration of all the viewing enjoyment I had given him over the years, he could give me $200 for the lot!

"It was 5:00 p.m. now, and I was still $100 short. Chase banks are as ubiquitous as Starbucks, so I had a lot of options where to *deposit* the money. But to *get* more money, do I go uptown? Do I go downtown? I only had to come up with another $100. Then I remembered . . .

"In 1992, I shot a documentary in Turkey and bought a chain in a gold factory. I had never taken it off, not because I love gold, but because it reminded me of a wonderful experience in my life. There was a jewelry store on the Upper West Side that had given me a good price on a necklace of my mother's. That's where I unclasped the chain for the first and last time in years and laid it on the scale. The offer was $145. Forty-five more than I needed. Maybe I could take the kid to a movie that weekend. I passed the cash over to a Chase teller at exactly 5:45. I'd made it!"

"Just in the nick of time!" I cheered.

"But I was living with a daily fear that I never want to feel again."

Millions of Americans live with the fear that Richard described. Their stories don't involve Turkish gold chains and uptown-downtown subway chases rivaling *The French Connection*. A vast number obviously don't make it to the bank by 5:45, or there wouldn't be so many people paying the usurious interest rates that Richard was racing to avoid. For most debtors this race never ends.

It didn't end for Richard that day either. He was telling me about his close shave in retrospect. If I'd met him at 6:05 that day, he might have reported the 5:45 victory briefly and gone on to tell me about the piano he was trying to sell on eBay ("Never got a single offer") to make sure he didn't fall into the 29 percent rate the next month.

"What kind of racket is that?!" Richard demands. "Twenty-nine percent interest rates while your money in the bank is getting less than 1 percent! Well"—he calms down a little—"at least I kept my American Express at 15.9 percent, the Visa is 19.9 percent. But chipping down that debt once you've accrued it, that's the hardest thing I face now that I'm stabilized."

This is how Richard Bey finally stabilized himself.

"At that point I had a $600-a-week job and a $1,200-a-week rent. So I decided to move into a studio apartment. I was going to do it in the same building because that way you don't have to put down a new deposit."

"To avoid the cash gap between putting down the new deposit and getting the old one back?" I asked.

"Right. That's the kind of thing I was constantly thinking of. How do you avoid laying down cash for a deposit? How little can you spend for dinner in this restaurant? Is it worth it? Which is cheaper? That kind of thinking, every single day.

"But Richard," I said, "we all think that way every day."

"After a certain point, for me at least, you have to turn it into a game of how little can I spend today, or else . . ." He shook his head at the thought of what constant economizing might do to one's soul.

"So I looked at a studio apartment in the same building, and I told the woman I'd be by the next day to pick up the lease. Then I showed up for work. Three-quarters of the people weren't there, and the rest were crying. The guy had pulled the plug on the whole operation.

"The person there said if you do your show today, you're not going to get paid for it. I said, 'I've already done the research.' But even as I'm on the air, I'm thinking, 'I'll never get another job around Christmas unless I'm going to be Santa in Macy's.' "

"Did you ever think about those kinds of jobs?" I asked. "Santa? Messenger?"

"Not even when I was an actor."

"Good," I said. "Because you can't just pick them up today the way we could in our day."

"Anyway, it wouldn't solve my problem."

So Richard gave up on moving halfway down to a studio apartment and moved all the way down to his parents' condo in Florida. The hardest part about that was telling the child, he said. But Richard had temporarily solved the school problem, and he promised to return often. Indeed, he manages to crash in New York about ten days a month.

Richard's parents had left their condo mortgage-free, and he and his brothers maintain it as a vacation home. But moving, even to a free place, takes money.

"When I was an actor, I moved from sublet to sublet by just tossing my stuff in the car. Now I have all these physical possessions." Richard remembered another resource. "I have a friend who was a vice president of MTV. I see him once a year. I hadn't touched him yet. So I went and explained that I had to get out of New York and I couldn't even pay for the movers.

"He said, 'Just tell me how much you need.' I said, 'I think I could do it for $2,000.' He said, 'I'll give you $5,000 but only on one condition, that you never bring it up; you never think twice about calling me as a friend because you owe me the money.'"

"That's just the condition I would make," I said. "Because if you're embarrassed to call me, I'd lose a friend by helping out."

"Unfortunately, I *am* embarrassed to call him," Richard said, laughing. "But I called the woman who lent me the $1,000 and said, 'I've stabilized, and I can pay you $200 a month. She said, 'That's all right. I don't need it right now.' My friends are motivated by friendship and trust, like I was with Bill. Are they as foolish as I was?"

As part of the stabilization process Richard decided to start collecting his union pension early. It was an old-fashioned guaranteed-benefit plan to which his broadcasting employers had paid in over the years.

"I'm collecting $3,800 a month. That's $44,000 a year." Richard had been a high earner. "Most of that goes to paying down my credit card debt. If I could have waited till I was sixty-five or sixty-six, I would have had a $6,100-a-month pension. With that and Social Security, I would have been golden. Still, God bless the union."

"You know something," I said, "somebody might say that $44,000 a year and a fully paid-off apartment on the ocean is not a bad way to be ruined."

"You don't have to bring 'somebody' into it," Richard answered. "I say that myself. I could have had a lot worse places to start from or to have fallen to."

"Do you think this might be a transition into retirement?" I suggested cautiously.

"Last time I spoke to Bill—I'm pretty sure I'm the only investor who still talks to him—he was worried about going to prison. I said, 'What are you going to get, three years? Two with good behavior? What you should do is lose weight, work out, bring lots of books.' Then I realized, what I'm telling him to do in prison is what I'm doing in Florida. I work out an hour and a half a day. I eat frugally. There's a place that has a twelve-inch pizza for $7.95

on Tuesdays. I eat half of it Tuesday and the other half Thursday. And books. It used to take me two months to finish one. Now two a week. I call it a pleasant purgatory. Pleasant because of the walks on the beach. Purgatory because it's a waiting room till I figure out how to get back to New York and do something creative."

"I bet you will," I said and thanked him for his time.

But Richard Bey is used to being the moderator, not the moderated. After collegially answering my questions about his personal experiences, he took the mike, so to speak, and gave me a general wrap-up of my subject.

"I'm not an economist, but this is my theory. Since the seventies, middle-class workers, their wages haven't gone up. There's lots of statistics on that. You can fill them in.

"People don't realize this, because it was hidden first by the dot-com technology boom. That was the time when even a chimp could pick a winning stock. In fact they had a chimp on television doing it. So stocks went up, and everyone thought they were rich. When that bubble burst, they had the real estate bubble. People said, 'Oh my God, I'm living in my bank. Every day I get richer just because I own a house or a condo.' Then that burst. So now people are waking up to a reality that's existed since the 1970s. The earnings of the richest 2 percent have increased eightfold—*eightfold*. We haven't had a disparity of wealth like that in this country since the Gilded Age.

"So what they've basically done is moved all the money out of the middle class with a shell game. They stand there and say"— Richard transforms himself into a street hustler behind a table with three cups—" 'Your money is under your house.' " He lifts the first cup. " 'Whoops, no, it's not there.' Okay, your money is in the stock market. 'No, it's not there.' So where is all the money? 'The money is under the third cup and that's my cup. And not only that, but if I lose any of it, the government's going to put it back for me.'

"I tell you, if anything would drive people to socialism, it should be what's going on in this country right now. Myself, I happen to be a capitalist because I believe incentive is very important. I believe that hard work, dedication, talent, perseverance, all of those things should be rewarded. But what we have now is the law of the jungle. The lion eats everybody because he can."

Thank you again, Richard Bey.

The last time I saw Richard he was enjoying a six-week sublet in Manhattan while he guest hosted a morning show for Sirius Radio. Then it would be back to pleasant purgatory. His friend and fund manager Bill pleaded guilty to defrauding the German bank and is free till his sentencing, but the one-armed treasurer is fighting the charges. So far no money has been distributed to investors. But the fund's assets, Richard fears, are being depleted by managers and lawyers. Richard is active in the investor committee to get the SEC to stop what it considers new mismanagement.

Chapter Fourteen

THE PERFECT TWOFER

Author Gets Insulated

I live in a low-income building in one of the wealthiest parts of Manhattan. Westbeth consists of 383 rent-stabilized apartments in a rehabbed nineteenth-century warehouse with tall, leaky windows right on the Hudson River. Heating costs us a fortune.

That's one reason I noticed that the $800 billion American Recovery and Reinvestment Act (ARRA), or "the stimulus" as it was more often called, included $5 billion for weatherization.

Insulating old buildings seemed like a perfect recession twofer. It yields immediate energy savings and creates jobs that use the very skills that were idled when home construction crashed.

Since 1976 the U.S. Department of Energy has run the Weatherization Assistance Program, which channels relatively small amounts of money through state governments to nonprofit community groups to subsidize the weatherization of low-income homes and apartments.

Much of the $800 billion stimulus was to be distributed in the form of tax cuts to private businesses and grants to state and local governments. But the increased weatherization money would go to those community groups to pay workers to produce a public good.

It wouldn't put millions of the unemployed directly on the government payroll the way the Works Progress Administration (WPA) did during the Great Depression. But it was as close to the WPA as anyone dared go this time around. So aside from a personal interest in replacing my leaky windows, I had a professional interest.

I imagined myself interviewing a formerly unemployed young man from the Bronx—no, make that a young woman—her electric screwdriver poised in midair while joyful neighbors wave their lowered utility bills.

In order to locate such direct stimulus beneficiaries, I set up an appointment at an established weatherization group in my area. But I found this message on my answering machine: "We had a meeting today at two o'clock, but . . . I was told by my funding source that I needed to request, um, that you needed to request in writing, um, the organization that you're working for and pretty much what you're interested in because I have to submit the request through DHCR's [Division of Housing and Community Renewal's] media office."

When I phoned back, she promised to send my written request for an interview off to Albany *tout de suite*. We'd reschedule just as soon as she got the approval. "It's nothing personal."

After a few frustrating weeks I gave up on appointments and dropped in at some outer-borough community groups where sweet, sincere people either didn't know or didn't want to tell me how they were going to spend their weatherization money when it came through.

I began to suspect that something ugly like a jurisdictional struggle was holding up the works. Then I happened to attend a lecture on alternative energy. I recognized one of the speakers as a staff member at a community group I'd tried to visit. After her talk I privately mentioned my interest in weatherization, and she implored me not to tie her environmental activism to her community group. But why shouldn't a weatherization worker champion alternative energy?

That's when I realized that I might be feeling the Van Jones effect. The man President Obama appointed as his "green-jobs czar" had recently been outed on Fox Television as a 1960s black radical—which indeed he had been. Fox ran pictures of him sporting a huge Afro and saying things he would surely put differently these days. Within a week the president accepted his resignation.

Fear of tarnishing the weatherization program with environmentalism or radicalism was one worry. Corruption or the appearance thereof was another. Over its two-year duration the stimulus bill would provide small groups with enough money to insulate about a million homes a year, or seven times what they'd been doing until then. That's far more than these groups were used to spending. To avoid scandals, real or cooked up, they adopted elaborate paperwork to account for every penny. I wonder if the WPA got off to a slow start like this. I still wanted to write about people finding work, but I put weatherization on the back burner.

Then, one day about a year and a half later, I saw a Hispanic man in his twenties, a white woman in her thirties, and a black man in his forties eating bag lunches behind my building. Next I spotted them on the roof measuring the emergency doors, then in the basement near the laundry room. Finally, the trio knocked at my own apartment and asked permission to install new bulbs, faucet sprays, and weather stripping.

While I'd been writing downbeat recession stories, my building management had slogged through a weatherization application. To be eligible, over 66 percent of the tenants had to have incomes not more than 150 percent above the official poverty income. (So that's why they'd collected our Social Security numbers.) Once we'd been declared poor enough, we were given an energy audit to determine what upgrades we could use.

Now my personal insulation team, José Santos, Tracy Leonardo, and Cleavon Bell, were at the door. Tracy, the clipboard woman wearing boots, tool belt, and ponytail, explained their mission. I let them in, and they dispersed with choreographed speed toward the bathroom and the kitchen. By the end of the afternoon almost every apartment door on my floor had one of those silver strips to hold in the heat.

I caught Tracy without her clipboard one lunch hour, and she joined me for a cup of tea. An organization that prepares women for nontraditional employment helped her to find her way to the weatherization group. "I was the first girl they ever hired as a field worker," she said.

Before that she'd worked as a plumber (nonunion, noncertified), a bartender, an emergency medical technician, and at an animal hospital. Along the way she'd earned a BA in criminal justice. "I thought I wanted to be a cop till I dated one for a while." She'd also gotten a law degree that she's never used.

"Does your family feel disappointed that you have a law degree and you're doing construction work?" I asked.

"They wanted me to get a degree; I got a degree. My dad is a carpenter. His career was computer technician at IBM. But he redid our entire house. He can do it all, and he taught it to me. I love it. Besides, I make more at this than I would as a lawyer."

For the moment that was probably true. The Davis-Bacon Act of 1931 required contractors receiving federal funds to pay local "prevailing wages." This is generally interpreted as union wages.

After a bit of a tussle, that requirement was attached to the ARRA or stimulus bill.

Because of the variety of work they did, my three insulators were classified as carpenters. That meant that Tracy had earned $70,000 during the year that she'd worked exclusively on stimulus contracts. "I paid like $15,000 in taxes," she told me proudly.

But the two-year stimulus program was just about over. Because of the slow start her group was granted an extension to finish our job. But in another few weeks she'd be back to earning $40,000 a year. That was fine with her, she said. It was still the work she loved.

Though Tracy was clocked out for lunch, she took a call from Cleavon with a question about washers. "Yes, I'm the informal supervisor," she acknowledged when she got off the phone. "Except not in the sense that I would ever rat the fellas out for anything. But I tell them what to do, where to go next." This was not because of her education, she said, but because she'd been taken on staff a little before them.

Her really important contribution to the team, Tracy thought, was helping them get into the individual apartments. This was tricky in any part of the city. "But frankly," she said, "gaining access in your building is harder than anywhere else I've worked." That's all she would say. Despite my coaxing, her professionalism prevented her from telling me stories about my eccentric neighbors.

She did wonder, however, whether the heating team would have as much trouble when they came to put regulators on our radiators. "They're going to be installing in each apartment," she said. "But it'll be a bit of a waste because of the windows."

That's when the bad news sank in. A building like ours has to pay at least one-fourth of its weatherization costs. Replacing hun-

dreds of irregular-sized windows over a century old was beyond
our means. It would be so expensive that it probably wouldn't meet
the government's standards for cost effectiveness even if we could
pay our share. So after the job was finished, I'd still have to stuff
towels into the cracks around my elegant, wood-framed windows
when it rains. Tracy deplored the energy waste even as she admired
the vintage woodwork.

She thanked me for the tea, noticed my odd-sized hanging lamp
on her way out, and promised to send up special flood bulbs that
would fit. In her capacity as informal supervisor, she also promised
to send "the fellas" up to talk to me next day at lunch.

José Santos is a slight twenty-four-year-old born in the Dominican
Republic and raised since school age in New York City. Weatherization work introduced him to many new neighborhoods, and he
didn't mind sounding provincial. "I went out to your supermarket
the first day to buy sandwiches for us. It cost $30. We bring our
lunch now." José's partner Cleavon Bell is a sturdy forty-five-year-
old who seems far more sophisticated and confident. But they both
felt awkward being interviewed.

"Is the ARRA money the best pay you've ever earned?" I asked
the two.

"Is that the Recovery Act?" Cleavon asked.

"Yeah," José answered him.

"Then yes," Cleavon said, laughing, "because I *recovered*. We
started to be like real citizens. We got a taste of what it was to pay
bills, to have money in your pocket."

"Yeah, it feels good," José agreed.

When I asked if they saved any of the temporary windfall, they both answered by describing how they were now helping their families. José talked about paying his mother's rent. Cleavon spoke about his children's Catholic school tuition and his sister in college. "Everybody is eating now," Cleavon said. "My wife says, 'You know, you're the number one son right now.' I'll have to break the news to them when ARRA stops," he ended wistfully.

Though they hadn't really answered my question, I surmise that for good or for bad just about all of their ARRA earnings flow directly from their pockets into the consumer economy. Indeed one of the advantages they cited of ARRA jobs was that they paid weekly instead of biweekly.

"Before this job," said José, "I used to be a porter near Avenue B. I had nine buildings, and it paid me minimum wage. Like seven twenty-five an hour. They took me on like full-time, but they didn't tell me that it was temporary. After a couple of months they started giving me days off and more days off. I'm asking them, 'Is it my work?' But actually, it was because they only needed a weekend porter. Some weeks it was a $50 check. That wasn't enough, because I got . . ."

"We got families, responsibilities," Cleavon said, finishing José's thought.

"So I had to quit."

After that José was hired on a house renovation. That also paid minimum wage, but the boss was nice and taught him some carpentry skills. But the renovation was soon finished. Then a friend of the family's showed José a flyer about the community group that offered GED and job training, and he registered.

Cleavon, by contrast, had had a longtime, steady job with a private sanitation company. "I decided to give it up after twenty years. It was outside in the weather, and it was having its effect on my body. I decided to take a different turn of direction, go to school, take a trade. This is why I choose to learn this trade of 'going green.' "

"Going green slash carpentry," José said, carefully stating their current occupational designation.

José and Cleavon both earned GEDs and were both among the few accepted into the community group's internship program at $8 an hour. They were among an even more select group taken onto the weatherization staff.

"We learned a lot," Cleavon said.

"We learned too much," José interjected.

"They pay us for using our brains," Cleavon continued. "We do a lot of physical work, but we also got to always figure out how to do things easier. 'Work smarter, not harder.' "

"I suppose you have to use your brains to get into some of these apartments," I said, fishing.

"And your charisma and personality," Cleavon responded with a dapper smile.

"You must have to keep lists of the appointments you make and the way different tenants responded when you knocked on their doors." I was still hoping for gossip about my neighbors. But the fellas didn't bite either.

"Yes, paperwork is very essential," Cleavon explained. "If you don't have the paperwork correct . . ."

"Then it's like you haven't even done the job," José said, completing what must have been a maxim of their training. "Remember the first week," José said to Cleavon. "Everyone said, 'Not yet. Let them do the physical work, but don't let them touch the paper-

work.' But Tracy, she showed us and let us actually do the paperwork from the first. Tracy, she taught us the ropes."

"This crew, we're like family," Cleavon said.

"We *are* family," José said, making it stronger. "We see each
other every day; we help each other. Staff is family."

When the community group hired people directly, it sent us a mul-
ticultural team that looked like the squad room on a NYC cop
show. But it also subcontracted work to profit-making companies. These minority-owned businesses tended to be monocultural,
though serially diverse. We had a team of Russian electricians who
installed fixtures. They generally answered tenant queries by saying, "You ask super." The Russians were replaced by a team of
Mesoamericans who spoke less English but managed to communicate benevolence.

I had the most contact with the West Indian heating crew
because I have a work space above the heat return lines and the
building was getting brand-new oil burners. We would soon have
hot water instead of steam circulating in our pipes.

One day one of the heating men asked if I knew how to locate
the person who rented a room that was always locked. Their clipboard guy, a trim, confidence-inspiring man who was informative
but not chatty, explained that they'd been trying to trace a pipe
into our wing. The building was once several separate structures.
Unfortunately, there are no complete plans documenting all the
jerry-rigging that had been going on since the nineteenth century.
The pipe they were after exited one building section from the first

floor but was then directed sharply upward inside a three-foot-six-inch brick wall and may have entered our area through that always-locked studio on the second floor. That turned out to be the case. The place was full of mysteries like that.

I would sometimes see the heating men in animated conversation at the end of a hallway. They were now working for me, and we employers are always suspicious that workers are discussing personal matters on our time. But whenever I managed to overhear anything, they seemed to be talking about pipes and elbows.

Except for a core of salaried men, contractors generally hire people as the work comes in. The clipboard man told me that since they'd started our job, his company had hired two recent community college grads plus a master plumber—now laid off. They'd also brought back some regulars.

A mature man who worked off and on installing heat sensors told me that back in the islands he'd been a factory engineer and also taught at a college. He hoped to find that kind of work in New York, but till the recession is over, he said, "This is my survival job."

A young American black man I'd not seen before emerged from the basement one day with sweat-soaked work clothes. I felt guilty pestering the tired fellow as he sank down onto the step and took a drink from his thermos. But he seemed happy to talk about his job. He said he'd been with the company for three years. He'd been off during the prior three weeks, but they needed him now to rip out these big old oil boilers.

"Yes," he confirmed, "it's always off and on like that, but it's a really good job." I asked what he does in between. "I hate doing nothing, so I volunteer at churches and stuff . . . No, I'm not married. I'm concentrating on work first." He had no special training for the job. "I'm a laborer, but learning lots of things as I work along."

It was good to know that he wasn't making $7.50 an hour the way José had when he picked up construction work. Laborers had to get the union laborers' wage on jobs covered by the Davis-Bacon Act.

"We have to keep track and make sure to change wage scales when our people work on government jobs like weatherization," the clipboard man explained.

"Then I shouldn't be taking up your expensive stimulus time with these questions," I apologized.

"I'm on salary," he said with a slightly sardonic nod. "I wish I was hourly." Then he checked something off on his clipboard, excused himself, and headed to the basement. That's the last I saw of him. I went away for two weeks, and when I returned, our weatherization was complete. I miss having those purposeful well-paid workmen around.

Did the weatherization stimulus work? It obviously created jobs for both experienced and new construction workers. And since these men (Tracy was the only woman I encountered) tended to spend their pay, the money had the multiplier effect planners hope for from a stimulus.

We won't be able to tally the energy savings either nationally or even in my one building for about a year. Everyone is keeping before-and-after records, for, as Cleavon and José learned, "if you don't have the paperwork correct . . . then it's like you haven't even done the job."

At this point I can only report anecdotally that before we were weatherized, apartments facing the river were chilly, while I had to keep my windows open to let the heat escape. Since that's no longer true, it's reasonably safe to say that our weatherization must have produced *some* energy savings. Assuming it was run efficiently, it was indeed a twofer. It both created jobs and lowered our utility bills. We're also releasing less carbon into the atmosphere. So if you're concerned with global warming, you might call it a three-fer.

There are still millions of drafty houses in America, and we needed a much larger jobs program to have a Keynesian effect on recession unemployment. For these reasons I ought to favor extending the weatherization initiative. And I would, except for one serious drawback. We paid for it with borrowed money.

"Don't Borrow, Take!"

When you borrow money, you have to pay it back with interest. When the government borrows, the money flows from all taxpayers to some investors. It's true that Treasury securities were earning relatively low interest at the time, but a billion here, a billion there, it adds up.

In my populist fantasy, bringing insulation to urban tenants was akin to electrifying rural households through the New Deal. There's one big difference, though. The Roosevelt administration didn't fund its projects by leaving rich people with all their wealth and handing them more.

Between 1929 and 1939 taxes on capital gains rose from 12.5 percent to 30 percent; taxes on the top bracket of earned income rose from 25 percent to 79 percent. Not only did a U.S. Congress impose these redistributive taxes, but even more amazingly, rich people actually paid them. Like it or not, they chipped in to fund the New Deal.

But between 1976 and 2008 the capital gains tax went *down* from 39.9 percent to 15.4 percent. Then, in 2010, two years into the recession, it went down a further four-tenths of a percent. Instead of asking people who arguably caused the mess to chip in for the cleanup, we're paying them interest on the cleaning bills. Those cleaning bills include the $800 billion financial bailout. So we paid banks interest for the money we borrowed to give to them.

Yes, I'd like to see more stimuli like weatherization. But if we pay for them by borrowing, then the rich get richer. Piles of investment capital grow at a time when there are still few productive ways to invest. But that led to the last bubble and will inflate the next one that much sooner. That's why I offer the practical advice: "Don't borrow, take!"

Unfortunately, those were not the options on the floor. The U.S. Congress wasn't choosing between debt-funded stimuli (borrowing) and tax-funded stimuli (taking). At the height of the crisis its debate had been between insufficient stimuli and no stimuli at all. We'd had our insufficient stimulus bill. Now, with twenty-four million officially unemployed or underemployed, Congress had decided to try no stimulus at all.

(Actually, there was a third option I hadn't noticed. As the special weatherization stimulus program expired, the government cut back the regular Weatherization Assistance Program that had existed since the Carter administration. So you might say we've opted for a *counter*-stimulus.)

CONCLUSION

Down Is a Dangerous Direction

Not Your Normal Crisis

Economists describe recessions as either V-shaped, meaning sharp down, then sharp back up; U-shaped, where the economy muddles around at the bottom for a while; or W-shaped—that's the dreaded double dip. The Great Recession was experienced as a classic V by my three investors, but it morphed into an L for the Pink Slip Club Four, who live on wages.

That may sound like the way the world works. "There's nothing surer," as the old song says, "the rich get rich and the poor get poorer." But oddly enough, that eternal verity is usually suspended during recessions.

During normal-shaped recessions, companies tend to maintain their plants and retain their core workers while they wait for business to pick up. In the meantime (in between time), they compete on price and take less profit.

As a result, the share of national income that went to investors used to decline during a recession, while the share that went to employees increased. I'm not trying to tell you that workers got rich during previous recessions or that the rich became penniless like Richard Bey. But their shares of the total income took a temporary Robin Hood turn.

This time it's been different. Corporate profits were 25–30 percent higher at the official end of the Great Recession than before its onset. Meanwhile, wages as a share of national income fell to 58 percent. That's the lowest the wage share of income had been since it began to be recorded after World War II. The *Financial Times* (my source for these statistics) calculated that "if wages were at their postwar average share of 63 percent, U.S. workers would earn an extra $740bn this year [2012] or about $5000 per worker."

Investors not only took a bigger share of the current national income during the recession years; they also found themselves in possession of more of the accumulated national wealth.

According to the U.S. Federal Reserve Bank, the middle class (the middle 60 percent of us) lost a greater percent of its wealth during the Great Recession than either the poor or the rich. By 2010 the wealth of the median American family was lower than it had been in the 1990s. The Federal Reserve calculates that about three-quarters of the recession wealth loss was due to the housing bust. That makes sense since homes are where working Americans store the bulk of their wealth and their children's inheritance. And during the recession, homeowners lost equity and entire houses while investors, like it or not, took possession.

To understand how this wealth shift plays out over the generations, I got back to my GI coffeehouse friend Duane, or rather to his family.

Duane's children walked away from their inheritance because it was underwater. Whatever money their father put into the Arizona house was washed away when the bubble burst. I asked Duane's son about the history of home ownership in his family.

He knew that his grandparents owned their home in Cleveland and that Duane's sister moved in after both grandparents died. But he didn't know much about the financial details, so he put me in contact with his aunt Claire.

I was surprised and touched by the things Claire remembered hearing from her brother about the GI coffeehouse. "That was forty years ago," I demurred. But Duane had talked about the place so much, his sister responded, that "you'd think he got his honorable discharge from the Shelter Half [the name of the coffeehouse] instead of the army." That made me feel bad once more about how I'd let our contact drop.

Claire filled me in on the days after Duane's discharge when he came back to Cleveland.

"It was a kind of shitty time in the family," she remembered. Her father, a welder, was out of work. "It started off as a normal layoff. Most years he was off a few weeks for retooling. But this one stretched out. Being home all day waiting meant he got involved with everything going on in the house. Our dad, well, let's say he had a lot of opinions.

"Anyway, the way I remember it, Duane was hardly at home because that's when he met his wife. Dad had his opinions about her too.

"No," Claire said, "there was no big fight, just irritations. The whole family stayed close. Mom adored Duane, and he stayed especially close to my daughter. But it happened to be the first of the long layoffs for my father, and it was probably a good time for Duane and Sue to leave Cleveland."

Though their father's unemployment affected the mood of the home, it never threatened the ownership. "It wasn't like today," Claire explained, "where you have all these bills to juggle. Losing the house was not on the horizon for my folks. Of course they may have tried to hide their worries from us, but as far as I know, even refinancing was never on the menu."

According to Claire, their father served in World War II and bought their home on the GI Bill. When their mother died, Claire and Duane inherited the place free and clear. Since Claire and her husband lived in Cleveland and were ready for a larger home, they took out a mortgage to buy Duane's half. It came to about $65,000.

Duane put all or almost all of the money into the first house that he and his wife bought. As far as Claire knew, he transferred that equity from house to house each time he picked up stakes.

"It's too bad for his kids that he landed up in Arizona at the peak of the market, but real estate was never my brother's reason for relocating anywhere. Duane wasn't interested in scenery; he wasn't interested in real estate. It was always about work he liked where he could keep learning. He always said he wanted to—

"Keep ahead of it," Claire and I said simultaneously, echoing Duane's old refrain.

"He was a supervisor on that last job," she wanted me to know. "He might have been the only person he supervised; it was a small place. It had to do with lasers."

"So," I said, bringing us back to real estate, "your parents owned a house they could leave to their two children free and clear, and now one of you owns a house that you can . . ."

"Half a house," Claire corrected me. "We paid down most of the loan for Duane's share, but then we took money back out to help my daughter through college. Let's say that my parents' whole house was converted into a third of a house and a teaching degree.

"It's too bad for Duane's kids about the Arizona house," Claire repeated. "But we probably won't be able to leave a house either. My husband used to work where they had a company pension, but we don't have that now. I don't see how we can retire without selling or somehow taking the rest of the equity out of this house. I like to think that what we passed along to our daughter is a way to earn her *own* living and buy her *own* house."

I assured Claire that she and her husband obviously passed many valuable things to their daughter in addition to a formal education. But it remains true that one couple in the grandparent or World War II generation had a house to leave free and clear. Two couples in the next generation will have somewhere between zero and a third of a house to leave.

It may not be entirely fair to say that the siblings moved down in the world or that Duane and his sister "lost" one and two-thirds houses during their working years. But it is fair to say that the current generation of investors owns one and two-thirds more houses. They may not know how to get cash out of them right now, but investors will emerge from this recession owning more of America. The generation that includes Claire's and Duane's children will inherit less. They'll probably earn less too.

Not Your Normal Recovery

I mentioned that during past recessions employers tried to maintain their plants and keep core workers. It was basically a holding operation. But right in the middle of the Great Recession, Big Box went ahead with a major time-and-motion study designed to get more work out of its warehouse hands in the future. The Boutique didn't just put its saleswomen on short shifts. It used the recession as an opportunity to get rid of its entire commissioned sales staff. As business picked up, returning shoppers were welcomed back by low-paid part-timers.

Normally, salaries are low at the start of a recovery and gradually rise. They may rise "anemically" or "haltingly," but the direction of recovery is up. But during the three years since the official end of the Great Recession in June 2009, median family incomes went *down* by 4.8 percent. Black family income declined by 11 percent.

In the spring of 2012 families with these lowered incomes increased their borrowing. This phenomenon was headlined on the financial pages as a sign of "returning consumer confidence." Before the recession people borrowed to buy houses they couldn't afford. In recovery they borrowed to buy cars and educations they couldn't afford but felt they needed in order to find jobs. Is that a sign of consumer confidence or consumer desperation?

In 1929 the United States plunged from a peak of economic inequality into the Great Depression. A decade and a half of political and labor struggles resulted in significant redistribution, and we exited World War II on a leveler and more prosperous road.

By 2007 we'd reached another peak of inequality and plunged again. But unlike the Great Depression, the Great Recession didn't narrow the wealth gap for even a moment. For all our bruises we merely went into a deep pothole and emerged on the same rough and dangerous road.

Wages are down, borrowing is up. Investors have emerged from a V-shaped recession, while the low line of wage earners' L seems to extend indefinitely. That might mean that we're in an unstable recovery with more potholes ahead. But there's another way to interpret it.

When American companies began moving manufacturing jobs overseas in the 1970s, the idea was to make products more competitively for the American market. Today, American CEOs impress potential investors with their foreign sales figures and their plans to open new markets abroad. *The companies that wrote us off as workers now write us off as consumers.*

If you're not a worker, not a consumer, and you don't earn significant income from investments, then you don't have much of a place in capitalist society. In the course of this recession millions more of us have slipped into that no place. Most of us will still manage to eat and keep our televisions connected. But it can't be pleasant to live in a country whose elite have no regular use for us.

In Decline?

The phrase "jobless recovery" gained currency in the 1980s to describe what seemed then like an oxymoron. In the decades that followed, however, our recoveries routinely ended with a smaller percent of the population in the labor force. But once output is up and portfolio wealth has rebounded, the crisis is officially over. If you look at it that way, the horizontal line of our L is neither an extension of the Great Recession nor an abnormal-shaped recovery. That low line is the new norm.

The limbo bar will be set lower after each recession, and Americans will just have to contort themselves to squeeze under. This is inevitable, according to an increasingly mainstream assumption, because the U.S.A. is in decline.

Aspiring politicians don't usually announce that their nation is past its glory days. I suppose that's why reporters at a Bloomberg View breakfast in June 2012 perked up when former Florida governor Jeb Bush said matter-of-factly, "We're in decline." Columnists from both *Slate* and the *New York Times* took Bush's almost parenthetical comment as a sign that this son of a president and brother of a president was no longer a contender. But while politicians rarely say it, our financiers and industrialists not only think but act upon it.

What a reversal! When I met Duane at the GI coffeehouse, we peaceniks were considered anti-American. We denied it then and I deny it now. Still, there were usually a few on any antiwar march who anticipated the empire's decline and may even have gloated.

Today it's not our protestors but our corporate leaders who anticipate American decline. And while they may not gloat, they certainly hedge their bets. The thinking seems to be "We're in decline; there'll be less to go around; *I* want as much as ever, so *you'll* just have to take less." Or, more primitively, "I'm getting mine while the getting is good."

Are they right? Is our long-term decline inevitable? I tend to think not. But frankly I don't know any better than they do.

I do know, however, that a nation doesn't have to be the world's supreme industrial power nor have its largest economy (however that's measured) for its citizens to live comfortably.

During the decades when America bestrode the world like a Colossus, many nations peeked out between its legs—producing, buying, selling, and dividing the profits. The nations that divided them the most equally, the cradle-to-grave welfare states like Germany, France, and the Scandinavian countries, also had the most productive economies. During the Euro currency crisis (another top-down financial innovation), the nations with the greatest inequality happened to have the most fragile economies. Yet the fix so often prescribed for us is austerity for the masses and incentives for the rich. In other words, even greater inequality.

How many more recessions and jobless recoveries can we cycle through? How many times can we emerge with the rich richer, the poor poorer, and more of the middle class marginalized? Are there any inherent limits to inequality? What happens to a market economy when all the money winds up in one pocket?

It's Time for a Jubilee

A child who's beating his parents at Monopoly knows that the game will end if he gets *all* the money and *all* the properties. But the more he gets, the more he gets. If he wants to keep playing past his bedtime, he has to find a way to slip some money or houses over to the other sides of the board. But that's not that easy to do, at least not if you stick to the rules. If he really wants to keep the game going, the child will have to cheat.

Throughout history, societies have faced economic paralysis when too much wealth wound up in too few hands, so they invented cheats to keep the game going. American Indian communities practiced periodic redistribution rites like the potlatch. Ancient Babylonian kings issued occasional debt cancellation decrees to counter the tendency for all the good land to fall into a few hands. The ancient Hebrews prescribed debt cancellation and land return every forty-ninth year. It was called a Jubilee.

For four decades a variety of corporate and governmental policies converged to transfer wealth from the poor to the rich. As a result, workers developed a need to borrow, and investors had an even more desperate need to lend.

This has played out as forty years of "innovation" in the financial world and as anxiety and exhaustion in the daily lives of American families who took on more jobs and more debt. It's time for a Jubilee.

TO BE CONTINUED . . .

How do you end a book about people whose lives are still up in the air? None of the recession sufferers we spoke with in *Down the Up Escalator* were hungry, and only one was truly homeless. But most of them couldn't be sure where or when they'll work, how long they'll be able to stay in their homes, whether they'll ever be able to retire or to have a baby, and more generally what will happen next.

Uncertainty is painful to human beings (and to other species too, I suspect). I can't quite bring myself to leave people I got to know personally—not to mention millions of others—in such distress. So I've created a Web site that we might call the ongoing book on the ongoing recession.

A book eventually gets printed. But no deadline stops me from getting back to individuals to find out how they're getting along. Their updates, taken together, may also give us some idea how the country is getting along.

You can catch up with the folks you met in these pages at www.downtheupescalator.com.

INFLUENCES, DEBTS, AND LOVE

I subscribe to the *Financial Times* and the *Left Business Observer*—two surprisingly well-written publications. Despite their different takes on capitalism, they almost always come up with the same statistics about the current economy. Those are the figures I most often cite in these pages. The *Financial Times* is a salmon-colored paper available at newsstands. To subscribe to the *Left Business Observer*, go to: www.leftbusinessobserver.com.

While writing this book I attended Professor Richard D. Wolff's monthly Update on the State of Global Capitalism (see www.rdwolff.com). Wolff's forthright Marxist analysis highlighted the fatal folly of lending to workers instead of paying them sufficiently.

From the very start of the Great Recession, economists including Joseph Stiglitz and Paul Krugman described it as a crisis of insufficient demand. They struggled against a sea of pseudo truisms to show that the kindly policy response would also be the hard-nosed and effective one. Economists from URPE, the Union for Radical Political Economics, did the same in their circles.

None of the economists I've mentioned agree entirely with each other nor are they responsible for my conclusions. But this unusual collection of credentialed economists who happen to speak and write clearly gave me confidence in my own observations.

I feel a twinge of guilt whenever I use the figures 99 percent or 1 percent, because so many other people did the collective work of making statistics about inequality mean something. Thanks to the folks I spent time with at Liberty Square and to others who occupied Wall Street and elsewhere.

Despite the vicissitudes of the publishing industry, great books will always emerge somehow. But books like mine would not be written without passionate, literate, traditional editors like Gerald Howard and old-fashioned, on-your-side agents like Joy Harris. Thank you both for keeping on.

Friends who know my darling husband, Frank Leonardo, wonder why I don't thank him for his support and inspiration the way other authors thank less deserving spouses. Frank loves me no matter what I do or don't accomplish in the world, and he shows it. This unconditional love inspires me to sit comfortably on the couch for hours. Without it I might write more, I suppose. That's O.K., though. I love him back the same way.

Salutations, in order of age, to Miriam Zissel, Chaya Mushka, Stefan, Menucha Rachel, August, Alice, and Rifka.